Eruptions of Inanna:
Justice, Gender, and Erotic Power

Eruptions of Inanna: Justice, Gender, and Erotic Power

Judy Grahn

A Sapphic Classic from
Nightboat Books
& Sinister Wisdom

Designed by Nieves Guerra

ISBN: 978-1-64362-076-3

Cataloging-in-publication data is available
from the Library of Congress

Nightboat Books
New York
www.nightboat.org

Sinister Wisdom, Inc
Dover, FL
www.sinisterwisdom.org

Contents

Introduction

Six thousand years ago, at least, people settled along and between two Mesopotamian rivers, the Euphrates and the Tigris, in the area called the "Fertile Crescent." A rich civilization, Sumer, grew there, lasting thousands of years and producing lively agriculture, trade, arts, and sciences, including the art of writing. In addition to records and accounts, Sumerians excelled in writing down their mythology, songs, and praise poems. The earliest poet known by name is Enheduanna, a high priestess in the city-state of Ur. She wrote three long poems about her own exile and suffering, while exalting Inanna, the goddess of love, beauty, justice, and so much more. Sumerian poets, nearly all anonymous, praised their pantheon of major gods in written language; none has had more lines of poems survive the ages than the goddess Inanna.

My retelling of eight myths about Inanna written by Sumerian poets beginning at least 4260 years ago are at the heart of this book. I am enthralled by the lush qualities of the poetries and intriguing plots of the stories of Inanna, but, as a poet myself, there are other reasons I am drawn to understanding this work. I see, in the ancient Sumerian poetry, pre-biblical roots of justice, gender, and erotic power.

Even as a child I was a spiritual person, called on to read my poetry in Bible class, and given a handsome Bible by my parents. As I grew older, I was beyond dismayed by the Bible: first by the exclusion of homosexuals from categories of sacredness; then by the absence of female presence in divinity; then, as I became more socially conscious, by the definition of light as "good" and dark as "bad" (in the New Testament especially), which only exacerbates social and psychological divisions. Later, I also became acutely aware of the split between human beings and the rest of nature, a split I learned did not exist in indigenous religions and practices. What accounted for all this, and what could be done, became major explorations of my life. What can be learned through reading literature that preceded the Bible, and in important ways fed into its wisdom? And what was left out that we could value now?

Every once in a while, if you are lucky, someone bursts into your life and turns it 180 degrees in some marvelous direction. This happened to me in 1984, when Betty De Shong Meador asked to work with me, bearing the gift of the poetry about the Sumerian goddess Inanna. She brought this initially as the present of a recently published, bright red volume of translated work by the poet Diane Wolkstein and the Sumerian scholar Samuel Noah Kramer: *Inanna, Queen of Heaven and Earth*. I had been writing woman-centered poetry for twenty years, most recently traipsing after a modernized version of Helen of Troy, but the mythologies recorded by the Sumerian poets describing the lively exploits of this goddess of love and war took the pressing subject of women's contributions to culture to a whole new level.

Betty, as a Jungian psychoanalyst, had a keen eye for the psychological value of this work, especially as it recast notions of women's autonomy, emotional depth, leadership abilities, erotic power, and capacity to find value in periodic depression and renewal. We were both transfixed. Then coming into a class I was teaching, Betty reached much deeper during the next fifteen years as she devoted herself, alongside a Sumerian translator, to rendering into English comprehensible and beautiful poetry by a woman named Enheduanna, born some 4300 years ago in the Sumerian city of Ur, about the goddess Inanna. Betty published the gorgeous translations, along with her excellent commentary, in her book *Inanna, Lady of Largest Heart: Poems of the Sumerian High Priestess Enheduanna.*

Eruptions of Inanna adds my poet's interpretations to Inanna's major stories, each one revealing a different aspect of how her poets viewed her unique approaches to dispensing justice. Inanna's womanly powers include the arts and crafts of her civilization, fates of her Sumerian people in life and afterlife, welfare of the land and its plants and creatures, and her clever use of menstrual rules. I explore how the Sumerians modulated intense states of energy; and how Inanna used erotic energies, her multigendered joyful processions, and other methods of interconnection, such as taverns, to create a lively civic life. Inanna also had a volatile nature; I compare her stories with the central plot and lessons of the Bible's Book of Job, exposing some of the more contentious language associating Inanna with war and revealing an expanding scientific understanding of the Sumerians, while also exploring gender-changing capacities attributed to Inanna. The well-known myth of King Gilgamesh and his quest to overthrow Inanna and gain for himself the secret of eternal life recounts an important story about two very close male friends with a rejecting eye toward the sacred feminine; from this story, the roots of three worldviews about life and death, all of which we grapple with today, emerge. These three worldviews are the paradise myth, reincarnation, and secularism. Inanna's character recurs and erupts in Akkadian, Babylonian, Greek, Roman, north African Gnostic, German, and contemporary American poetic mythology. Tracing eruptions of Inanna through history invites new ways for readers to reimagine our world today.

Over a nearly thirty-five year collaboration, Betty Meador and I had hundreds of conversations about the qualities attributed to Inanna, the meaning of her actions, and the sacred, powerful presence of both female and transgendered characters in the original stories. In reimagining these ancient stories, what are most fascinating and valuable are the poets' perspectives on a clash of worldviews, and the ethical teachings implicit in poetry describing Inanna's relationships with both people and nature, crucially important for the challenges of our world today.

The myths featuring Inanna were written down between four and five thousand years ago by poets and scribes. The main characters are gods of Sumer. Enki is Inanna's grandfather, and god of "sweet waters," especially of the rivers and irrigation. Ninshubur is Inanna's fiercely loyal assistant and a goddess-queen in her own right. Dumuzi, whose name became Tammuz later, is Inanna's lover, and he is both shepherd king and bull god. Ereshkigal, goddess of the underworld, and of regeneration, is Inanna's older sister. Their stories and many others were composed by Sumer's great poets and inscribed on clay tablets; they survived over thousands of years, baked in fires, buried in dry sand. They date from 3100 BCE to about 2100 BCE, and reflect the beginnings of our own age of cities, agriculture, and industry.

A scholar's eyes collect intricacies of information and a range of interpretations; a poet's eye may see a different set, adding further value to the treasure that is Sumerian literature.

1
Inanna, Goddess of Justice

Inanna and the Errant Gardener: A Story of Justice

Inanna, the queen of heaven and earth in ancient Sumerian cosmology, has a very cool, wise grandfather, Enki, god of wisdom and sweet waters, who is often looking out for her. Portrayed as an older man with a long beard, Enki is a master gardener and water-management engineer; he also loves creatures and at this time is preoccupied with teaching a raven how to be a farmer. Enki has helped the people of Sumer establish a maze of irrigation ditches that run alongside plots of land planted with wheat, barley, figs, palm, lettuce, and other crops. The small fields are watered with a wooden machine called a *shadouf*; it catches the water, flowing along the ditch directly from the river, in a huge bucket that is attached to a long, curved, flexible pole with a counterweight, allowing the bucket to swivel on a tall base. Water from the irrigation ditch can be lifted gracefully and poured over the field. Enki is teaching a clever blue-black raven to place the tender sprouted seedling of a palm tree into the ground and then water it by working the *shadouf*. A raven doing the work of a man: "Who had ever seen such a thing before?" the poem "Inanna and Shukaletuda" asks.

Meanwhile the young shape-shifting goddess Inanna—the planet Venus to the Sumerians, but also taking earth forms, such as "Mistress Falcon," among other descriptions—has decided to turn herself into that swift bird and do some high flying over her lands. She wants to do more than just inspect them; she also is looking for any signs of injustice that need to be corrected. "She

7

went up into the mountains," according to the ancient stories, "to detect falsehood and justice, to inspect the Land closely, to identify the criminal against the just."

The poem has no trouble describing Inanna's own authority: she "who stands . . . as a source of wonder." She is dressed with a cloth wrapped around her hips, a special cloth that contains some of the powers that keep the world running. She acquired these powers from her grandfather after she came of age and decided to visit him in his temple, as told in a poem called "Inanna Meets the God of Wisdom."

Enki graciously had invited Inanna inside and served her honey cakes and beer. They sat and drank together; they drank and drank together, quite a lot of beer for quite a long time. After a while, Enki, feeling very warm and generous, began to recite the powers that he held—he recited them several at a time, and whenever he paused young Inanna raised her flagon of dense dark beer and said, "I'll take them!"

The *mes* (pronounced "mays"), the powers of the world, included the crafts, given one at a time: the arts of the woodworker, copper worker, scribe, smith, leather maker, fuller, builder, reed worker. Another set listed various priestly and related roles, including "the cult prostitute." Rituals and heightened senses were also given to her, as this poem excerpt describes from her own point of view:

He gave me truth
He gave me descent into the underworld
He gave me ascent from the underworld . . .
He gave me the perceptive ear
He gave me the power of attention

Emotions were included in the *mes*: fear, consternation, dismay, joy. And the *mes* assign various positions required for staffing the temple: incantation priests, libation priests, princess priestesses, and so on. Some of these cosmic laws are contradictory: the kindling of strife, and also counseling.

He gave me heart-soothing.
He gave me the giving of judgments.
He gave me the making of decisions.

Fourteen times Enki and Inanna repeated their ritual of drinking to the list. The very last powers were those of judgment and decision, and when Inanna said, "I'll take them!," all the powers passed over to her. Meanwhile, her venerable grandfather had passed out on his couch.

Inanna packed all the powers into her vehicle, the "Boat of Heaven," referring to the crescent moon shape, and accompanied by her assistant, the goddess-queen Ninshubur, set sail across the sky. The two were happily rocking away in their crescent-shaped shining boat, when far below them, Enki awakened. In alarm, he called for his assistant. "Where are my cosmic powers?"

The assistant said, "My lord, you gave them to the young woman Inanna."

Enki could hardly believe he had done such a thing. "Where is the power of attention? Where is the making of decisions?"

"My lord," repeated the assistant, "you gave them to the young woman Inanna."

Enki shouted, "Go and bring the Boat of Heaven back to me!"

Obeying Enki, the assistant set out into the sky to regain the powers from the goddess, using his own wizard forces. Inanna's second in command, however, who was also known as the

"Queen of the East," was a force to be reckoned with. Ninshubur was the daughter of the wind couple Enlil and Ninlil. An unmarried virgin, in her own hymn she describes herself as "august minister of the universe," and a "personal god of the Land," and "faithful minister" to the old Stone Age deities of the wildlands of hunting and gathering. One fragmented poem of Ninshubur's has lesbian overtones: "I will make the young lady, Inanna, born in the shining mountains, rejoice. I, the Lady . . . will make her rejoice." The word "rejoice" occurs in Inanna's love poems, referring to sexual pleasure and orgasm. Ninshubur is identified with the planet later called Mercury, the messenger, and she is also a shamanic warrior who had been taught ecstatic trance as part of her lineage as a child of the wind. "I, like my mother, I will fly high in joy like my mother," she sings, "I ride high in joy!"

When Enki's assistant sent his weapons to the prow of the Boat of Heaven, Ninshubur engaged them immediately. Everything he threw at her in the way of giants, thunder and lightning, monsters, ghastly forces, and terrible illusions, she thwarted and threw back at him. They went round and round like this six times, until Enki's assistant gave up, and Enki, again the gracious grandfather, acknowledged that Inanna as Queen of Heaven and Earth deserved the cosmic powers and was capable of dispensing them. She and Ninshubur sailed their Boat of Heaven to the dock of Inanna's city, where the people turned out in high jubilation, with drums and horns, to celebrate their victory.

Sometimes in the night sky you can see the two of them, bright Venus and the smaller shining Mercury, riding together in the silver glow of the crescent moon, the Boat of Heaven.

Now, as a more mature Inanna prepares to change her form, she dresses in a cloth that contains seven of the cosmic powers, wrapping it tightly around her hips. She goes up into the mountains and grows from her shoulders the wings of a falcon, to go on flying over her lands in an inspection tour, searching, as she says, for what might be false, or crooked and in need of adjustment. Beating her beautiful falcon wings, Inanna rises into the air, soaring from one end of the land to the other, from the jagged mountains to the gleaming rivers, from the broad grassy steppe to the dreadful desert and the sweet fruitful valleys. She dips and swoops, focusing her falcon eyes, until she grows extremely tired. Deciding to rest, she lands beneath a Tree of Life, the great golden spreading Euphrates plane tree, "whose roots tangle with the horizon of heaven," and, with her mind on her shepherd king lover, the bull god Dumuzi, she falls deeply asleep.

Meanwhile, a callow young gardener named Shukaletuda, whom we immediately learn is incompetent, has been standing in a nearby garden plot. His job is to water the plots, but none of them have any plants because he has pulled them all up. He is watching the east and west horizons, seeing the exalted gods. A sandstorm blows up, and, as he rubs sand from his eyes, he sees a goddess approaching, "like a ghost." Inanna circles and lands under the Euphrates plane tree.

He approaches as she sleeps, pulls aside the cloth with its seven cosmic powers over her genitals, and "had intercourse with her and kissed her." Then he returns to his garden plot.

When Inanna wakes with the rising sun, she "inspected herself closely"; she inspects her genitals. She considers what should be done, "what should be destroyed" because of her genitals.

The myth does not call this rape, as we know it in mainstream contemporary culture. The gardener soiled her vulva clearly, but probably a greater transgression was his crudeness, pushing aside the seven cosmic laws, "the great divine powers" woven into her loincloth, and underestimating the powers of the sacred feminine. She arrived "like a ghost," and he transgressed the body she was inhabiting at the time. As a mortal he could not do harm to the goddess, but he acted wrongly. She goes looking for him, to judge his behavior. When she can't find him, she unleashes some of her powers.

First, Inanna commands attention from the whole human community. She floods the land with blood, to the point that the wells and rivers are full of it. When servants go to draw water from wells, their buckets fill with blood. The irrigated orchards are drenched with blood. "When will this end?" people ask in great distress.

Inanna says, "I will search everywhere for the man who had intercourse with me." Still, she cannot find him. He has fled with his story to his father's house. Inanna then mounts a cloud and sends a fearsome storm flood. As she crosses the desert, she is accompanied by a sacred cross-gendered temple shaman (called a *pilipili*) and seven times seven other helpers.

Again the errant gardener, who has been hiding in fear, goes to his father and tells his story. The father says, "My son, you should join the city-dwellers, who are your brothers. Then she will not find you in the mountains."

Once again, Inanna takes action. She raises one of her magical implements and blocks off all the roads. The people cannot travel, and their entire economy shuts down. Still she does not find the young man who violated her.

She "directed her steps" now to visit her grandfather, Enki, who is in charge of the *abzu*, the central place of reality. She tells her story to him, adding ominously that she will not sit down quietly until she finds her transgressor. "Someone must make up for what happened to me!" she says. "I will not return to my shrine until you have handed that man over to me from the *abzu*." Sensibly, Enki immediately agrees. He says, "All right!" and "So be it!"

Inanna stretches herself across the sky "like a rainbow," and although the gardener, alone and frightened, has made himself as small as he can, she finds him. He relates his story, as he had previously, about being responsible for watering plants but acknowledges that he had pulled them all up, and they were dead. He says that he had sexual intercourse with her as she slept. Inanna now shames him. Since the text is broken here, perhaps she is saying that he isn't any better at the arts of sexual love (or anything else Sumerians were expected to do) than an ass, a dog, or a pig. This story has opened with Inanna's grandfather teaching a raven to chop up kohl, mix it with oil and water for fertilizer, place it in a hole the bird dug, plant a sapling palm tree in the hole, and water it by means of the *shadouf*. The contrast of the incompetence and carelessness of the young man with the skill of even a raven amplifies the gardener's failings. Inanna now stands fully in her judgment.

She declares, "You will die." She then says, "What is that to me?"

These chilling words don't actually specify that Inanna herself kills him, but they do make clear that she has withdrawn all of her benevolent love and approval. Unlike those she favors, he will not be reborn. Rather, as she tells the young man in a bitter condemnation, his soul will wander alone in "the palace of the desert." Moreover, his misuse of her will not be lionized or empowered in any way. Instead, shepherds will sing a sweet song about him, a song that furthers Inanna's province of love and sexuality as beneficial to women, men, and the land.

Inanna's love poetry celebrates her vulva, source of sacred power. "I rule with cunt power," she says, "I see with cunt eyes." Poetry about Inanna's love for the bull god Dumuzi makes it clear that sexual pleasure for the woman is primary, a prerequisite that precedes the male's pleasure: "When he treats me tenderly on the bed, then I too will treat my lord tenderly." She instructs him precisely how to satisfy her: "when he ruffles my pubic hair, . . . when he lays his hands on my holy genitals." The erotic power of the deified couple promotes vivacity, health, and abundance in creatures and people alike, serving as a model for her human charges. They too "thrive in the goodness of love" under her beneficial blessings.

Because of the primacy of the appropriate use of eroticism, the errant gardener's transgression is more encompassing, more about harming the whole Sumerian society, than is our narrow definition of rape as individual and devastating to the victim. A goddess, especially one as powerful as Inanna, would not be personally harmed by a human being. He is the one who is frightened, running away, hiding, and "from fear . . . he tried to make himself as tiny as possible." He is the one who is shamed and suffers lasting consequences and loss. She *inspects* her vulva and finds the evidence of his act. She is not hurt in any human sense; she is outraged that he is not acting appropriately. The myth emphasizes his incapacity to relate to the plants, to the land, and to the sacred feminine. He casually pushes aside the cloth around her hips that contains the principles of the cosmos. The myth conflates all these transgressions, testifying that anyone so careless with his own sexuality would be equally careless with everything else that matters. In other words, his fault is much greater than our concept and experience of the personal trauma of rape. At the same time, her solution does not empower him in any way, and it strips him even of his wrongdoing.

While his father advises him to hide among young men in the city, Inanna captures the gardener because she is able to use women's collective capacities to bring the entire society to a screeching halt, and because her grandfather understands her power and wants everything in his domain to function smoothly. This is the story of Inanna and the errant gardener.

Sumerian Culture, Everyday Life, and Connections to India

Fascinated by the poetry and stories of the Sumerians, I continue to learn about them. Sumerian culture is breathtakingly ancient, extending from earliest small settlements in 6500 BCE until the fading away of Sumerian language around 500 or 400 BCE. This six-thousand-year period of continual history covers the development of settled agriculture and herding, with the building and sustaining of some of the earliest known urban life, in the Fertile Crescent, what is known in our age as the country of Iraq.

Around eight thousand years ago, a lively people changed their way of life from the nomadic Stone Age with its brilliant stonework, basketry, pottery, and shamanism. Instead of wandering as hunters and gatherers, they settled between two great rivers that emptied into a marshy interface with the sea and created a permanent fixed economy based in horticulture of grain, fruits, and vegetables, mixed with herding and fishing. They were especially known for their productive crafts, creating trade driven by highly skilled artisans working with mining and metallurgy. With a more settled life, sciences and technologies could flourish, amplified by the keeping of records with marks on clay tablets, which after a few centuries became writing. Thousands of these tablets lay buried until the twentieth century, when archaeologists, following biblical clues, found them. Translations revealed a wealth of literary stories, poems, tributes, prayers, and the revelation that many biblical references and stories directly descended from, and drew from, the Sumerian poets.

The free market of Sumerian trade, with its possibility of both wealth and ruinous loss, was mitigated by the temples, which held enormous power, serving as community centers for gathering goods and taxes and redistributing them to people in need, even sometimes paying ransom for those captured in battle. Each temple housed one or another of the city's god or gods, and each city had unique deities; for example, the city of Uruk belonged to Inanna, while Ur was dedicated to the Moon deities Nanna and Ningal. Inanna's city of Uruk was the largest settlement in the world until Rome, achieving a population of 50,000 people at its peak. South of this, and also located on the Euphrates River, the city of the poet-priestess Enheduanna was Ur. With its tall mountain-shaped temple, called a ziggurat, Ur belonged to the Moon deity Nanna, even though Enheduanna fell in love with Inanna and wrote long poems as an exaltation to her brilliant light in the evening sky.

In general, however, Sumerian temples used an interesting cross-gender system: priests served goddesses while priestesses served gods. Sumerian life was socially stratified with a wealthy upper class of priests and kings; special status was given to musicians, poets, scribes, sex priestesses, and highly skilled craftspeople. Artisans formed a middle class, producing finished trade goods; artisanal families guarded the secret skills and recipes, passing the occupation down from father to son.

Sumerian cities were usually located on or near one of the two rivers, Euphrates and Tigris. As a result, boats and then ships were crucial to trade that spread all the way to Egypt and to the Indus Valley in what is now Pakistan and north India. Donkeys carried goods into mountainous areas, so the trade spread into what is now modern Turkey in the north as well as west to the Mediterranean Sea.

The poor, who wore a single cloth garment, might be forced to become indentured servants or even to sell a family member into slavery to get the family out of debt. Slaves were also people captured in raids and, later, in wars. Enslaved people could own property and could accumulate enough wealth to buy their own freedom.

Sumerian people loved their family life; they washed and dressed for dinner, sat on chairs, ate at tables, had wine for dinner, drank in taverns, paraded in festive processions, played musical instruments and sang, and listened to their poets. They kept dogs, donkeys, and, later, horses. They had museums to retain a history of their past. Their children played with toys. The markets held seasonal fruits: apples, pears, plums, dates, figs, apricots, melons, cherries, and olives. Vegetables included cucumber and lettuces, peas, beets, cabbage, carrots, and turnips. For meat they had sheep, goats, and pigs, as well as such wild animals as gazelles, deer, and wild birds; they kept geese and ducks for eggs. The rivers provided fish, and the herders supplied cheese, cream, and milk.

Women, especially in the earlier millennia, owned houses, served as the earliest brewers, owned and kept taverns, and were doctors, dentists, and, of course, midwives. Both sexes wore lots of jewelry, although women wore more of the brilliant stone and metal ornaments, which were also a form of wealth. While during earlier periods women owned property and had rights, later they lost much of this freedom. Men worked in the fields, created irrigation and other technology, and were brickmakers and skilled metalworkers. The oldest kiln yet found is at Sumer, dated at 8000 years old. Bricks were fired in them, as were some of the clay tablets with cuneiform writing. Boys went to school; in general, girls did not, though the fact of women poets means girls did sometimes learn to write. To some extent, there was social mobility.

There were few trees or stones in the floodplain of Sumer, so houses were made of mud bricks or of the high, thick reeds that grew in the marshes. Some mud-brick houses had only one door, painted red to discourage demons. Windows were small to keep homes somewhat cool in the heat. The houses, one or two stories, were built around a central open courtyard, which let in light and air. Women cooked inside over open-flame stoves. Lamps burned sesame oil. People wore wool and linen clothing.

As mentioned above, each city had a temple where the particular resident gods were cared for by temple officiants. Later, each city also had a palace for the king and his family. The upper classes lived in these more spacious dwellings, and they had indoor plumbing by the mid-third millennium BCE. Especially talented artisans, as well as prostitutes, poets, and musicians, could become upper class.

The poor lived in small but very beautiful reed houses, round or rectangular. The door was framed by a sheaf of reeds bent into a roof and tied together at the top; these served to hold the doorpost, from which a woven door could be suspended. The twin reed sheaves with their round tops were an early symbol of Inanna as a doorway.

The presence of deities was everywhere, and these pious people would have been very careful in how they comported themselves, how they expressed gratitude and care toward the forces of abundance and possible disaster that surrounded them. That meant their piety expressed itself in extreme care toward nature, even as they developed the human arts of agriculture, animal husbandry, engineering, construction, astronomy, divination, mathematics, uses of the wheel, trade, writing that kept close records and also early written literature, and musical instruments.

The icons of deities were placed in tiny reed huts for a washing and feeding ritual known as "mouth-opening." This prepared the icon to "eat"—i.e., to absorb the energies of the offerings that were brought, and thus to be persuaded to speak to the devoted humans through their mediums. The major and earliest gods were elements of creation—the cosmos, as the people understood and defined it. Womb mothers of earth and sea who created life-forms; fathers of the sky, of the wind, and of sweet water. Another womb mother of human life and death reigned in an imagined underworld, married to a constellation in the sky. Thus the parameters of the Sumerians' world were stretched as large as these Bronze Age people could see and imagine. They grouped their deities into families with successive generations. First the cosmos was described: Nammu, the primeval Sea goddess, An the Sky god, Ninhursag the Earth goddess, Enlil and his wife Ninlil the Wind gods, and Enki the Water god (water was associated with semen, so he was a fertility god). The next generation of deities was named for, and represented, the major lights in the sky: Nanna and Ninlil, the Moon couple, and their two children—Utu the Sun god and his sister who was the third brightest light in the sky, known to us as Venus, the planet of evening and morning, Inanna.

Deities were credited with certain arts, processes, and inventions. It seems reasonable to suppose that gender was assigned to the creation deities because initially humans of that sex had affected the invention or comprehension of something in particular. For example, women were the earliest brewers and tavern keepers, so it follows that the deity of beer would be a female, Ninkasi. (Incidentally the beer was so densely nutritious it was often served as the main course for lunch, and was used to pay workers.) Men invented tools such as those used in the irrigation system, credited to the god Enki; men used plows, and the god credited is Ninurta, another male. Dumuzi the bull god in charge of sheepfolds had a sister, Geshtinanna, who was goddess of vineyards. Women were midwives, and the birth, death, and reincarnation deities were female.

A female deity, Nisaba, whose name meant "soapwort"—a cleansing herb used on altars if not also on icons—was credited with the art of writing, among other accomplishments. Writing in Sumer has been traced to a temple practice of people making tiny representations of their offerings—tiny sheep, for instance. These tokens, used to track temple offerings and debts, were wrapped in clay envelopes and stamped with shorthand representations of the tokens. These shorthand glyphs eventually became letters, pressed into clay tablets with an implement made of reed, the stylus. The Sumerians understood that when the stylus in one's hand trembled, this indicated the presence of the goddess Nisaba; we might call this trembling "inspiration." Poets sometimes ended their poems with "praises to Nisaba, goddess of writing."

But it was Inanna, goddess of erotic love, justice, nature, growth of plants, as well as both war and the arts of city life, who must have been the most beloved of Sumerian poets. Those writers left us more lines dedicated to her and her adventures than were devoted to any other god, and they ultimately exalted her as a primal creative force. In this sense, she is similar to Shakti, the Indian goddess of life energy. It may seem like a great leap of distance between the Tigris-Euphrates Valley and the Indus Valley of north India, some fifteen hundred miles away by land, yet less than seven hundred by sea, but it is not. These two great early cultures were trading partners, and shared cultural overlaps. "Lila" is a name for wind in north India, while the god of wind in Sumer was "En-lil," "lord wind." "Nona" and "Nana" are names for the planet Venus in north India, and my poet's ear hears a similarity to "Inanna." The Sumerian goddess has often been compared to the Hindu goddess Durga; both are associated with big cats (lion, tiger respectively); both are female warriors for justice, and both are associated with bulls.

In my four visits to south India, researching women's and goddess rituals in particular, I witnessed festivals and practices similar to those described in some of Inanna's literature from thousands of years ago. I occasionally draw from these parallels in order to more accurately interpret the ancient poetry. The Indians and the Sumerians traded more than worldly goods in their exchanges.

Some Sumerian stories were incorporated into biblical and other sacred texts and mythologies over the centuries following the disappearance of Sumer as a civilization. What tablets found in the twentieth century reveal is how much was retained, even though revised, in biblical texts, and how much has been missing.

The Descent of Inanna into the Underworld

One day goddess Inanna puts her ear to the ground and hears a call to go below on a journey. Always a flashy dresser, Inanna decks herself out carefully for this adventure, from a shining diadem on her head to a string of dark blue lapis lazuli stones around her neck and "twin-egg stones" on her breasts. Her torso bears a gleaming breastplate, and on her finger she places her gold ring. She wears her long queenly robe and carries a line and rod, which is a measuring tool. Before making her descent, Inanna calls her warrior pal Ninshubur to her side. "Come my minister who speaks fair words," Inanna says, "my escort who speaks trustworthy words, I am going to give you instructions and my instructions must be followed."

Here Ninshubur is addressed as both "minister," who carries a scepter, and "escort," who carries a mace. This makes her quite a mixture of authority, one part sovereign queen who speaks eloquently, one part butch warrior who speaks clearly and honestly.

"Beat the lamentation drum," Inanna instructs, and "wear a single simple garment in grief for me. Tear the skin at the corner of your eyes, and on your breast, and near your vulva." Then she instructs Ninshubur to visit three creation gods of the older generation, approaching one at a time, to ask for their help. First the Sky god, but if he won't help, then go to the Moon god, but if he won't help, go to Enki, god of sweet water. Only after delivering these instructions does the goddess Inanna approach the sinister door of the netherworld to knock at the outer gate. The gatekeeper leads her through seven gates down to the inner chamber, the domain of Ereshkigal, queen of the underworld.

The two goddesses are sisters, Inanna being the younger. Ereshkigal is in charge of death and rebirth, as is her daughter, Nungal. Inanna's favorite niece, Nungal is a deified midwife who uses her mother's powers to decide who shall be reborn. Among them this whole family is in charge of life-forms, Inanna having the benevolent upper-world powers of abundance, sexuality, and industry.

Inanna has clearly come to gain underworld powers that will enhance her reign and give her further maturity and authority. She certainly isn't powerful at this stage of her initiation, however, since by the time she arrives in her older sister's chamber, the gatekeeper has removed all her clothing, her jewelry, and the measuring line and rod, one item at each of the seven gates. He has also strictly enforced the rule that she must not ask questions; she must be silent. She is in a vulnerable state, being initiated into underworld powers.

Inanna's irrepressible spirit remains high in spite of all this, and she attempts to sit on Ereshkigal's wooden throne, whereupon the older queen slaps her. Inanna is described as "naked and bowed low."

At this heart-trembling moment, she is sentenced by a group of judges of the underworld, the Annunaki, who declare her "guilty!," then kill her and hang her body on a peg, where she is to remain for three days and three nights.

Now the scene shifts to the above-world, and to faithful Ninshubur, who has been in deep mourning, drumming, singing lamentations, tearing her clothing, her face, her breasts, and her vulva or upper thighs. Following Inanna's instructions, she has made her entreaties to the Sky god and then the Moon god, couching them in the metaphors of craftspeople:

> Do not let your daughter
> be put to death in the underworld . . .
> Do not let your precious lapis be broken
> into stone for the stoneworker.
> Do not let your fragrant boxwood be cut

The responses of the upper-world gods are both fearful and dismissive; Inanna wants too much, they say. Besides, no one returns from the underworld. When the Sky god and the Moon god refuse to help her, Ninshubur goes to the house of Enki, Inanna's grandfather. He is immediately concerned for Inanna and creates two non-gendered beings, the *galaturra* and *kurgarra*, who can easily visit the underworld. However, he cautions them not to be taken in by any offers of Queen Ereshkigal, or she will never let them go. One of them carries the plant of life, and one the water of life. They find Ereshkigal in a state of giving birth, and very irritated. They commiserate with her and she turns Inanna's body over to them to resurrect. Ereshkigal then gives Inanna the Eye of Death, the courage of truth-telling, for her own use.

In order to leave the underworld, Inanna must find someone to take her place. She begins her trip to the surface, accompanied by ravening demons who hem her in on all sides like sharp reeds. The demons first try to seize Ninshubur, who is still in her ragged sackcloth waiting for Inanna. The goddess stridently protects her. "Ninshubur . . . gives me support . . . gives me advice . . . she is my warrior who fights by my side . . . I will never give her to you." The demons move on to two more supporters of Inanna, and again she protects them.

Eventually the monsters of the below-world visit the palace of Inanna's lover, the bull god Dumuzi. He has been oblivious and apparently uncaring, sitting in a splendid robe on his equally splendid throne. Inanna turns her Eye of Death—true-seeing—upon him, declaring that he is the one who should go below to replace her. He resists, running off to his mother's house, disguising himself, but sooner or later he must face the music. His terror of the journey is lessened by his sister, Geshtinanna, who is in charge of the vineyards, volunteering to serve six months in his place, so he needs to go for only six months at a time. This part of the myth has long been understood as an agricultural depiction of the seasonal changes. Over centuries of time and a variety of cultures, Dumuzi as the dying lad gradually morphs into Tammuz and Adonis, Attis and Lado, mourned by women especially as the death of the grain god at harvest, then celebrated in his rebirth as the green sprouts of spring planting.

Inanna and Bilulu

A variant of the ending that sends a reluctant Dumuzi into the underworld for six months at a time produces a dramatically different story, one that is yet another example of Inanna's seeking and providing justice. So far, Inanna's outrage has been activated by an insult to her vulva as well as to the precious *mes* and the land itself; her ritualized, generational battle with her grandfather to prove she is capable of keeping the *mes*; and her capacity, on coming up from the underworld, to see clearly and speak the truth of judgment, even when the one who needs some correction is her dearest beloved. What would her reaction be if she lost that beloved altogether and had to deal justice to a gang of his murderers?

The story of Inanna and Old Woman Bilulu begins with Dumuzi's terror. After Inanna cast her baleful Eye of Death upon Dumuzi, and declared him guilty, saying he needs a trip to the world of shade, he goes into complete panic mode. No wonder! He is being dragged by the nasty underworld demons, who are already tormenting him, even kicking over his buckets of milk. He manages to escape and shows up at the house of Inanna's brother, the Sun god. You've got to help me, he begs. Turn me into a gazelle, anything, look, I am your sister's beloved. I gave her and you all kinds of gifts. I danced on her lap, I'm the one she loves. Turn me into a gazelle, please! You won't? Well, then turn me into a snake, please!

At this, the Sun god relents and Dumuzi slithers off in a new snake body to the house of Old Woman Bilulu, who he thinks will give him cover and a place to stay. But by running away from Inanna's judgment, he has given up his chance to go to the underworld, and thus to gain greater maturity in transformative resurrection.

Now the scene changes to Inanna, who is weeping for Dumuzi, obviously worried about him as he is missing from his sheepfolds and grainfields. Where is her sweet lover? She sings, using the repetition characteristic of much Sumerian poetry: " 'O Dumuzi of the fair-spoken mouth, of the ever kind eyes,' she sobs tearfully, 'O you of the fair-spoken mouth, of the ever kind eyes,' she sobs tearfully. 'Lad, husband, lord, sweet as the date . . . O Dumuzi!' she sobs, she sobs tearfully."

The myth describes Inanna as "fully apt and fully knowledgeable," as though the poet wants to emphasize that the goddess is not a kid anymore.

Soon after her lamenting song, one of the bull god's servants rushes up to her in a panic, to say that Dumuzi has been murdered and lies on the floor with his head smashed, in the house of Bilulu. He goes on to report having seen a man, a stranger, with Dumuzi's sheep, stealing the flocks away from their home.

On hearing this ghastly, devastating news, the first thing Inanna does is sing Dumuzi a second lament of appreciation, grieving over his loss just as, earlier, Ninshubur had grieved for the loss of Inanna while she was in the underworld.

Then, enraged at what has happened, bereft of her lover, Inanna seeks justice and goes to the alehouse near Old Woman Bilulu's dwelling. I imagine her in the dark interior of the tavern, hunched with elbows on a brick counter, sipping strong dark date-sweet ale from a huge clay jar, flashing fierce light from the corners of her eyes. Talking aloud to herself, Inanna declares that she will fix the fates of this gang of thugs. While she is at it, she will make a good resting place for her lost love.

At this point the poet asks dramatically, "What is in Inanna's heart?" and immediately answers: "She will kill Old Woman Bilulu, that is what is in her heart!"

Old Woman Bilulu, the head of her family and her "own woman," is talking to her dreadful son, a fieldworker who has left fields littered with the bodies of those he has killed while committing robberies. He is stacking up the bales of wheat and penning the sheep he has stolen from Dumuzi's stables and corrals. Also present is a third man, one who has no friends, is "child of no one." They are a little mob of outcast, murdering thieves.

When Inanna arrives, she declares with no hesitation, "I will kill you," to Bilulu, and "then I will destroy your names."

To Bilulu she says, "May you become the waterskin full of cold water that is used in the desert." With this, she continues, Bilulu will call Dumuzi back to life, if only for a moment, and gladden his heart. Using her powers to effect transformation, the goddess will turn the murderer into one of the most cherished implements of Sumerian life: a container of life-giving water. Bilulu and her son, Inanna decrees, together will become goddess and god of solace for lost souls in the desert, and wherever the need is, they will pour a libation, and scatter flour, and thus take care of those who wander in the barren terrain.

After this decree the goddess sings a third lament for her beloved.

Even though the characters appear wholly human in this story, they are also beings of nature: a shining planet who is a queen of heaven and sometimes a woman; a snake who was formerly a bull, a king, a lad, and sometimes a man; a waterskin of cold water, who started out as an old woman and is now turned into a goddess along with her thieving son, who has now become a god, consigned the task of ritually feeding the wandering dead to bring them momentarily back to life on earth . . . It's magical realism, Sumerian style. The conclusion is a new ritual: libation of water and a scattering of flour for beings wandering in the desert, especially for the lost lad. Presumably he would take his last visible form of a snake. And the intention of the new ritual, Inanna states firmly, is to make Dumuzi reappear in physical form, if only for a moment, and to give him joy, "to gladden his heart."

From then on, Old Woman Bilulu does gladden his heart, the poet says. As a last gesture, Inanna stretches out her hand to her beloved Dumuzi, who lies crushed on the ground.

Revenge for Inanna turns a bad deed into its opposite: something that produces joy. This alchemy of restorative justice is accomplished not through wishful thinking but rather through a fierce transformation and a change of ritual. For ordinary Sumerians, this story must surely have meant that any who held the teaching sacred would never, ever kill a snake. (A parallel practice of protection for cobras continues in goddess-influenced communities of India.)

One more story reveals how Inanna uses her *mes* to enhance civic life, empower women, and set a place for herself in the pantheon of deities.

The Cursing of Akkad

Eventually, by about 2200 BCE, the early, bountiful, more peaceful era of Sumerian civilization ended, and a military empire grew up. The general who led this new move was an Akkadian named Sargon, who founded a city named Akkad. In a later Sumerian poem, "The Cursing of Akkad" (translated by Joshua J. Mark), Inanna was credited with bringing particular gifts to this place:

> Holy Inanna did not sleep as she ensured that the warehouses would be provisioned; that dwellings would be founded in the city; that its people would eat splendid food; that its people would drink splendid beverages; that those bathed for holidays would rejoice in the courtyards; that the people would throng the places of celebration; that acquaintances would dine together; that foreigners would cruise about like unusual birds in the sky.

She filled the city with wealth, music, interregional trade, and a precinct specifically for women: "Holy Inanna established the sanctuary of [Akkad] as her celebrated woman's domain."

She also brought graces: "She endowed its old women with the gift of giving counsel, she endowed its old men with the gift of eloquence. She endowed its young women with the gift of entertaining, she endowed its young men with martial might, she endowed its little ones with joy." For decades, even the foreign lands were at peace during this time, and their people experienced joy.

Then, after Sargon's death, his grandson Naram-Sin became king. Inanna continued to free the trade ways until wealth poured into Akkad every day. There was such an amount that it caused "a weariness to the gates"! Despite her impact, Inanna had only a small throne space there. She could hardly receive all this bounty, and now began thinking of building her own temple to store some of it. But Enlil the Wind sent a message of disapproval at this further expansion (an encroachment into his own turf), and Inanna left, taking the city's "weapons"—which, as I will explain later, must have included, or even have primarily consisted of, *tools*—with her. Following her, the other gods withdrew their approval, Enki took away the wisdom and connection to the source of life, Ninurta carried off the jewels of office, the Sun god took away eloquence, the rain left, and so on.

Life in the sanctuary "was brought to an end as if it were only the life of a tiny carp in the deep waters."

The king then dreamed that Enlil would not allow the city to thrive, and he became depressed. For seven years Naram-Sin hung his head, gave away his robes of kingship, and tried to find out why Enlil had withdrawn his favor. He prayed and begged, he used auguries of divination—all to no avail. After seven years of this, enraged, he gathered troops, marched north, and ferociously attacked Enlil's home city, Nippur, and the temple where the god lived. He destroyed the walls, opened all the inner sacred chambers, tore out the drainpipes, ravaged the city. He loaded ships with the wealth of Enlil's city and, as the poet emphasizes, "as the ships moved away from the docks, the intelligence" of the king's own city "was removed."

Enlil, the great storm god, the Wind, immediately retaliated, responding to violence with violence. The god set in motion a huge invasion of Akkad by hill people who had never participated in Sumer's city life. They dismantled the economy, scattered the herdsmen everywhere, and blocked up the canals and docks, to the point that life was as it had been prior to the invention of farming and domestication of cattle and sheep, prior to trade and commerce. Dog packs in the streets attacked the starving people.

Meanwhile, in Enlil's own damaged city, Nippur, wise old men and women set up lamentations with drums for seven days and nights, young women tore their hair, and young men "sharpened their knives," as though to cut themselves in a show of grief. Priests showered the icon of the god with cooling water. Enlil settled down and slept. Nippur began to recover.

The other gods, including Inanna, sided with Enlil, cursing the city of Akkad for all time. Their curses were horrific, an apocalyptic fate the poem describes in great detail. The place permanently returned to the sparse state prior to urbanization—even the clay pots dissolved into formlessness—and became uninhabitable. The population perished.

The poem ends by praising Inanna for the destruction, as though she were deemed ultimately responsible for dispensing or withholding all the civilizing arts and crafts. Why would she aid in the destruction of all her own efforts, of her women's sanctuary, of her arts and graces?

Once again, a poet cast Inanna as goddess of justice. In this case, Inanna is aligned with all the powers of nature, of which

Enlil was, along with gods of the sky, earth, and waters, foundational. No human is to attack the fundaments of nature—the rest of nature will respond, and the "arts of civilization" will mean nothing.

This morality tale is not backed by historical evidence, even if it stands as a useful lesson for today. It's a vivid story of how (*not*) to deal with loss, especially loss of one's wealth, comfort, and stable situation. The amassing of wealth brought by civilization and industry, which is accompanied by the ceaseless expansion of comforts, along with the expectation that this will continue "forever," sets people up for equally massive disappointment, rage, and grief when the comforts stop. King Naram-Sin let his ego-rage rule by attacking the home temple of the god Enlil. Attacking, in other words, the Wind, and by extension all of nature.

In this sequence of five mythic stories of Inanna, the goddess of justice performs her tasks of maturation. She acquires the *mes*, the powers of the world, and the right to wield them. She learns to make judgments and fix fates, even of those closest to her. She uses women's blood power to protect their priceless sexual autonomy, as well as the well-being of the land. Resurrected after her perilous journey into the below-world, she wields the powers of life, death, and rebirth, becoming part of her cosmic midwife family. In the myth about Old Woman Bilulu, Inanna learns to turn personal tragedy into the best possible outcome: for the good of all, including creatures of the desert wilderness. And in "The Cursing of Akkad," we begin to get a sense of how the poets describing Inanna saw her in relation to the most powerful deities in the Sumerian pantheon, as part of the justice of nature.

2
Gilgamesh, the Rebel Who Turned Against Inanna

Inanna's poets gradually elevated her and embellished her accomplishments over centuries that ranged from early peaceful periods, through the more tumultuous rivalries among Sumer's city-states, and into an era of uneasy unification through establishment of an empire, that of Sargon I and his son and grandson.

Sargon's family empire lasted 160 years, and when it failed, a new culture took hold, building on top of the older one. As more people from the west and north came in, the Akkadian language supplanted the Sumerian language. People from the east, in the Zagros Mountains, attacked Sumer's cities, sacked and burned them, which helped preserve the precious literature by baking the clay tablets. A new empire arose, based in what started as a small city on the Euphrates, north of the Sumerian cities of Ur and Uruk. This new city, Babylon, reigned from the eighteenth to the sixth centuries BCE, a period of twelve hundred years. During the Babylonian empire, the water and semen god Enki was called Ea, and Inanna was called by her Akkadian name, Ishtar, and was greatly revered—by some. An important, brilliantly developed new story, which had begun in Sumer and was amplified deep into Babylonian times, described a new kind of hero, one who rejected her love and her way of life.

The Myth of Gilgamesh, "The One Who Looked into the Abyss"

Once there was a Sumerian king, Gilgamesh, who was three-quarters god, one-quarter human. After acquiring his kingship as a young man in the city of Uruk on the Euphrates River, he proved to be an arrogant and coldhearted ruler. He separated his subjects from their own families and cared only for himself. The entire council of gods was disturbed by this behavior and decided to create for him a friend he would love in hopes he would acquire empathy. They called upon a creatrix named Aruru, to make from clay a person just like Gilgamesh, a reflection of him, named Enkidu.

Enkidu lived at first in the wilderness, eating grass with the antelopes and knowing nothing of city life. Charged with initiating him, Shamhat, a courtesan-priestess of Ishtar, went with a hunter-tracker to find him and teach him some ways of Sumerian civilization. She guided Enkidu to Uruk, the city whose gods were the Sky and the goddess Ishtar.

> Come Enkidu, to Uruk of the Sheepfold,
> Where people are resplendent in wide belts,
> And every day there's a festival,
> And where strings and drums are played
> And the holy courtesans beautify their forms,
> Radiating sexual prowess, filled with sex-joy,
> At night they force the great ones into their beds.

Shamhat the priestess immediately seduced Enkidu and they had sex intensely for a week; she fed him food he had never known, bread and wine, and oiled him. Thus he became a Sumerian man.

Like Enkidu, Gilgamesh has beauty and sexual prowess. As king, Gilgamesh has been practicing the rites of first intercourse with brides. The first thing Enkidu does is to go to a wedding and disrupt this practice, confronting the young king. Enkidu and Gilgamesh begin their relationship with a wrestling match, testing strength on strength. Then they embrace, clasp hands, kiss each other, and become more than friends. They have been instructed by the women to hug and love each other. Their homoerotic friendship is obviously intimate, with kissing, embracing "like a wife" and "like a bride," deep loyalty, and emotional commitment. They are lovers. These men are not gay in the contemporary sense; they are sexual with each other and also sexually heterosexual, extremely so for Gilgamesh, whose palace contains a retinue of his women. As king, in order to have legitimate heirs he will of course need to marry a woman.

But already his beloved Enkidu was heartsick. Gilgamesh immediately wants them to go find and confront Humbaba, the longtime guardian of the forest. By doing this he thinks he will make himself a hero.

"Why do you want to do this? . . . his very breath is death," Enkidu wails. Gilgamesh wants to make a name for himself by fighting, even if it means dying. The king taunts his friend, "Only the gods live forever; as for men, their days are numbered. What are you, afraid of death? . . . let me walk in front of you." Enkidu relents.

Together, they commission the smith for weapons, swords, and adzes, and off they go, on a long journey to a forest of cedar trees guarded by the ferocious power Humbaba, which had kept people away through the ages. As they enter the forest, "they saw the great cedar mountain, home of the gods, and throne-base of Irnini," who is a manifestation of Ishtar, meaning that this cedar mountain is part of her domain.

Gilgamesh is devoted to the Sun god, who now comes to help the king's murderous plan, sending distracting winds; the two warriors attack the forest guardian, and Enkidu delivers the fatal blow. The two heroes cut off Humbaba's head. Then they go after what they call Humbaba's "henchmen," meaning the cedar trees, and chop them down.

After this slaughter, they return to Uruk. Gilgamesh washes up, combs out his hair, and decks himself in clean clothes and his crown. He is so handsome that Ishtar, upon seeing him, is attracted and proposes marriage, saying, "Give me the fruit of your body," and offering in return her gifts of abundance from the land.

Gilgamesh responds with sarcasm: "What could I give you, who already have the best of everything?" Then he insults her: "You're a cooking fire that goes out in the cold . . . pitch that defiles the one carrying it . . . limestone that crumbles in the wall," ending with "You are the shoe that bites the owner's foot."

His accusations hinge on his disappointment that she never gave "eternal love" to any of her lovers. Instead when she grew tired of them, she turned them into other creatures: one into a "shepherd bird" with a broken wing, and another into a stallion, one into a wolf, another into a frog. Gilgamesh mocks Ishtar, "You loved the stallion glorious in battle: / You ordained for him then the whip, the goad, the halter."

Furious at this slander toward her sacred office, Ishtar goes to her parents in the heavens and complains about how Gilgamesh has insulted her grossly. Although the poem doesn't say this directly, Gilgamesh has rejected the entire premise of human sexual engagement with her erotic divinity as enhancing the vibrancy of social life, the growth of plants and creatures, and the industry of people, producing abundance for all. She demands that the Sky god give her "the Bull of Heaven" and kill the rebel Gilgamesh. She threatens to open the underworld and set the dead to devouring the living if the Sky doesn't do as she wishes. The Sky complies.

The Bull of Heaven roars down upon Gilgamesh, but the two friends together surround and kill the bull, thrusting a sword into its neck behind the horns like the earliest of matadors. Now Enkidu and Gilgamesh are "blood brothers." They tear out the bull's heart and offer it to their deity, Shamash, the Sun god.

Ishtar, enraged, curses Gilgamesh for killing the bull. Enkidu goes further, taunting Ishtar by tearing off the animal's thigh and throwing it at the goddess while threatening, "If I could reach you, I would do the same to you."

At this deepest of insults, "Ishtar called together the hair-curled priestesses / the love priestesses and temple whores / and over the thigh of the Bull of Heaven she set up a wailing."

Gilgamesh hangs the bull's horns in the shrine of his ancestors and rides his horse down a public street, bragging loudly to the city's people, especially the women, how great and brave he and his buddy are.

The two men, proud of themselves, embrace, wash in the river, and return home to sleep. During the night, Enkidu is jerked awake by a nightmare. He dreams that the great creation gods, outraged at the murder of Humbaba, held a council, deciding that whoever committed this crime must die. That would be Enkidu, who struck the fatal blow. Even as he recounts the dream aloud, Enkidu begins to fall ill.

Angry at his weakness, which increases day by day, Enkidu curses all Ishtar's women, especially the sex priestesses of Inanna, and more particularly Shamhat, the one who first enculturated him.

The lines of his curse are shockingly familiar, beginning with a "stick that will beat you" and continuing:

You will love the child who beats you.
Your hungers will never be satisfied.
The shadow of the wall shall be your resting place.
The drunk and thirsty will strike your cheek.

The curse is so fierce the Sun god intervenes: "Why do you curse the women who gave you so much?" He placates Enkidu by promising that Gilgamesh will honor his name after he dies, and in brotherly grief will wander the earth dressed in the skins of dogs.

Enkidu calms down, and the Sun god blesses the sacred prostitutes; however, the curse also remains upon them.

Gilgamesh comforts Enkidu by telling about all who would be mourning him: the creatures, the meadows, the river, the trees, and the woman who first fed him and gave him beer, and oiled (anointed) him, and also the man who advised him. The king says, "They will tear out their hair for you." Enkidu dies.

Gilgamesh, in deep grief, avoids the usual death rites of the priestesses of Ishtar. Instead, he calls the artisans and has them make a life-sized statue of Enkidu of lapis and gold. Gilgamesh instructs the whole city to weep and direct their grief to the statue.

Gilgamesh repeats the story of his friend's life and their exploits together. He stays by the corpse for seven days, observing it: "I touched his heart and it does not beat." Then the young king throws off his royal clothing and wraps his own body in coarse animal hair and the skin of a dog.

Following Enkidu's death, Gilgamesh expresses his grief through outbursts of violence, which give him a certain satisfaction. Completely changed from his earlier cavalier attitudes, he now has become obsessed with terror over the prospect of his own death. In his wanderings, he becomes determined to speak to a sage, the one man known to have attained immortality. This man lives in paradise, on the island of Dilmun, far across the "sea of death." The king sets out to find the sage.

Gilgamesh journeys to the twin mountains that guard the coming and going of the Sun god and follows that course. After a long while, he comes to the dwelling of another manifestation of Ishtar, Siduri the Barmaid, or Tavern Keeper, "who dwells at the lip of the sea" of life and death. Siduri, interestingly, wears a veil. Her tools include a jug specially made for her and "the mashing bowl of gold" for fermenting grain for brew. (Another version of the story calls her "Woman of the Vine," who made wine for the gods.) Seeing Gilgamesh approaching with his dour, angry appearance, dressed in animal skins, hair tangled:

> The Barmaid looked into the distance.
> She talked to her heart . . .
> She took counsel with herself—
> "Possibly this one is a killer.
> Where is he headed . . . ?"
> Seeing him, the Barmaid barred her door.
> "I will break the gate down."

In response to his threat, "The Barmaid says to him, to Gilgamesh: / 'Why is your strength wasted, your face sunken? / Why has evil fortune entered your heart, done in your looks? / There is sorrow in your belly.' "

Gilgamesh explains that his dreadful demeanor has been brought about by grief for his friend and his own subsequent fear of death, explaining, "Shall I lie down like him, never to move again?"

Crucially, in an earlier Sumerian version of this myth, Siduri advises Gilgamesh to clean up and change to fresh clothing, then live everyday life, enjoying the treasures of food and drink and the company of a wife—"Let her delight in your embrace," she suggests—and children: "Pay heed to a little one who holds onto your hand." And this: "For love was granted men as well as death."

As the sad, angry, and frightened man presses for her help, Siduri tells him how to get to the boatman who could take him across the sea of death to find the sage Utnapishtim, the "one who knows about life and death."

First, she says, he will come upon a meadow filled with stone icons and a certain variety of snake living there. Then he will find the boatman.

When the volatile Gilgamesh arrives at the edge of the sea, he enters the meadow and goes on another of his rampages, crushing the stone icons and killing the resident snakes. Then he finds the boatman and roughs *him* up.

After this chaos settles down, the boatman, a large bird, smooths his rumpled feathers and informs the king, "You have killed the icons and snakes who enable our passage across the sea of death."

Gilgamesh does not respond, and despite this setback, the wise boatman thinks of another method, long poles with which they laboriously make their way for weeks across the deadly sea, finally to dock at the island of Dilmun, the paradise where Utnapishtim lives with his wife.

Seeing the face of the sour hero, Utnapishtim asks, "Why do you look so terrible?"

Gilgamesh again tells his sad story of losing his beloved friend Enkidu, this time adding his compulsion to study the corpse: "I sat by him until a worm fell out of his nose." And "six days and seven nights I wept over him." And "the one I loved dearly has turned to dirt."

Utnapishtim takes Gilgamesh in. Later the guest enviously asks Utnapishtim, "How is it that you, who don't look any different from me, gets to sit in the council of the gods?"

His host answers by telling "a secret of the gods," the story of a great Flood that once wiped out all of humankind except for him and his family. In the beginning, a long time ago, the elemental gods busied themselves for eons running the world. But after a while they became exhausted with the burden. Therefore they held a council. "We're tired and need some assistance," they all agreed. They decided to call on the creatrix Aruru to make a new creature that could help them. She mixed potters' clay with the blood of one of the minor gods who sacrificed himself for the purpose; with this mixture she made seven women and seven men, and thus there were human beings. The humans willingly proceeded to do some of the work of the gods, and for a while everything was balanced and fine. The gods rested, pleased.

But then, as time went on, the humans proliferated, becoming very noisy and quarrelsome. Enlil, the Wind god, was especially upset by their noise. He went to the council of the gods, which included Ishtar, to lodge his complaint, and they agreed to diminish some of the human population. They sent a famine, but the humans quickly recovered. So then they sent a plague. Again, a speedy recovery.

Enlil was aghast. "There are more of them now than ever!" he said.

So the gods discussed sending a great Flood. They "turned their hearts" in this direction, and swore one another to secrecy over this drastic plan. But the Water god Enki, now called Ea, was very close to his worshippers. He went to the house of one of them, whose name was Utnapishtim, and without—quite—breaking the secrecy promise, he spoke very loudly to the wall, "Reed wall! Reed wall!" He shouted, "You must build an ark," and "Abandon riches, seek life." He gave exact instructions for this boat—an acre square, seven stories high. On the other side of the reed wall, Utnapishtim overheard this, and followed the instructions, calling on dozens of artisans to come construct the huge vessel.

Once they finished, he loaded the ark with his wealth and all his relatives, along with seeds of every living thing around him, and animals of the fields. Finally, he herded on board the children of the craftspeople.

As the Flood storm began, it was dreadful—so dreadful even the gods were frightened. For seven days the shrieking torment went on, washing away everything. Ishtar cried out "like a woman in childbirth, that sweet-voiced woman of the gods." She went further in her lamentation, weeping for the humans as though they were children she had given birth to, crying regretfully, "How could I speak evil in the Council?"

Later, Ishtar and Ea/Enki placed the blame squarely on Enlil the Wind; they accused him of starting the Flood on his own, without adequate discussion among the council of the gods.

From within the ark, after the raging storm, Utnapishtim said he saw:

All of humanity was turned to clay . . .
The ground was like a great, flat roof.
I opened the window and light fell on my face.
I crouched, sitting, and wept.
Tears flowed over my cheeks.

Following the Flood, Utnapishtim and his wife were elevated to sit at times in council with the gods and allowed to live forever on Dilmun, the paradise island in the gulf near the mouths of the great rivers as they spilled their fresh water into the ocean.

While the myth doesn't specify what happened to the other survivors, presumably they proceeded to restore the human population. Enlil the Wind was especially upset that Ea/Enki had allowed a family to escape. And the elemental gods still had the problem of how to moderate human overpopulation. According to a different version of the story, called the Atarhasis, written about 1700 BCE, an explanation is given that includes *how* the gods brought human overpopulation under control. They created death, including infant mortality. They also established that some women would not be able physically to bear children, and they decreed special occupations for women, categories of priestess required to remain virginal throughout life. Perhaps this explains the practice of placing unwanted infants in reed baskets and giving them to the currents of the river.

When Utnapishtim ends his story, Gilgamesh is again in despair, asking him frantically where he himself could go, given that death was all around him. Utnapishtim agrees that death is everywhere, there is no escaping it. He has Gilgamesh washed and dressed in new clothing so the traveler, who had aged some on his journey, can now return to his city.

The host's wife intervenes, saying, "Look how our guest Gilgamesh has toiled and strained; what can you give him?" Utnapishtim softens and tells him about a secret plant, the plant of eternal life, lying at the bottom of the sea. Eagerly Gilgamesh ties stones to his feet and sinks to the bottom, where even though its thorns tear his hands bloody, he retrieves the plant of life.

Then he starts for home, and on the way he has his first generous thought: "This is the plant of Openings / by which a man can get life within. / I will carry it to Uruk . . . / I will give it to the elders to eat . . . / Its name is 'The Old-Man-Will-Be-Made-Young.' / I too will eat it, and will return to what I was in my youth." But on the way, he stops to take a bath, leaving the plant out in the open. A snake comes by, smells the flower, and takes the plant of eternal life away, shedding her own skin in a display of renewal as she goes.

Gilgamesh has lost the key to renewal, and by destroying the stone icons and snakes, he has ensured that no mortal will cross the sea of death to the island of paradise, Dilmun. He himself is no longer young and weeps for his condition. He admits, "I have not won any good for myself."

The king returns to his city of Uruk, "House of Ishtar," he says, praising the brick walls that he himself had once ordered to be built. Of Uruk, he says, "One part is city, one part orchard, and one part claypits," as though he has come finally to appreciate what a person is able to do in one life with whatever is at hand, rather than cutting down a forest and importing its wood, and then spending that life in fear of death's retribution.

Having lost the gift of eternal life from Ea/Enki's paradise, having spurned the goddess-barmaid's advice to seek family love, and having turned from the women's rites of reincarnation, Gilgamesh still wants one more chance to learn about immortality from his lost friend. Obligingly, Ea/Enki, the god of water, opens a crack in the underworld, through which the ghost of Enkidu issues for a brief exchange.

Earlier, Gilgamesh gave Enkidu explicit instructions for how to dress and act so as not to provoke Ereshkigal, the mother of the underworld domain, "who sleeps, / Her clean shoulders no garment covers, / Her breast like a stone bowl does not give suck." But as usual with these two rebels, Enkidu ignores all the women's rituals and consequently will never be reborn. The mother of life and death "does not let Enkidu rise again from the under-world" in fleshly form. Only his wispy ghost emerges on earth one last time, and the two friends vainly try to embrace. The advice Enkidu's ghost now gives the anxious king reflects their rejection of reincarnation, as he advises that of all the ways to die, the best is in battle, since the soldier will be revered by those who survive him. Then he gives a recipe for a man's happiness: a man with only one son wails in sorrow, one with two sons is a little better off, one with three has a treasure of deep well water, and so on, until the man with seven sons, who is so happy he is "like the gods." Aside from being remembered by one's son-survivors, there is nothing. Enkidu tells his beloved friend, "The body that you touched so your heart rejoiced . . . has turned to dirt."

This epic hero's journey ends with the idea of death as a finality.

Three Worldviews from the Myth

The Babylonian myth of a Sumerian king named King Gilgamesh contains three worldviews about the arc of human life and death. The tablets recording the original poems had lain buried for millennia in the sand and clay under new settlements built on top of the old cities. With their recovery and translations, and as original sources of viewpoints that developed over centuries into modern times, we could say that Sumerian poetry impacts everything in our lives today. Inanna (as Ishtar) played a huge part in all of them.

I have retold Gilgamesh's story using several sources, although most of the quotations are from John Gardner and John Maier's *Gilgamesh*. Throughout my retelling, I have carefully followed the plot, using my own words interpretively here and there. Like other Mesopotamian poems, it was lost to history for thousands of years, yet the essence of its lessons and archetypes continued in oral and written form—for example, in the Greek poet Homer's portrayal of the hero-warrior Achilles, who had a best friend to whom he was both emotionally and physically attached.

Contained within the Gilgamesh myth are three worldviews: immanence of spirit in nature, paradise as a mythic place of reward for pious behavior in one's life, and the rejection of both eventually resulting in secular humanism. All three have descended to us through the continual telling, retelling, and reworking of original Sumerian poems. Reincarnation is probably the oldest of these worldviews. The goddesses with their gifts of immanence of spirit and multiple kinds of love, including pervasive, aesthetic, magnetic, revitalizing erotic power, run throughout. Ishtar appears at least six different times in the Gilgamesh narrative, including in the form of the snake who makes off with, or retrieves, the plant of life. Ever dying and returning, cyclical life on earth belonged to the sacred priestesses with their midwife and birth goddesses, their underworld myth of death and resurrection, their snake of earth's vitality, and their rites of reincarnation, burying the dead with the clothing, jewelry, and food they would need on their journey to the next lifetime. This perspective merges human spirit with that of other life beings on earth.

The second worldview, that of paradise, revolved around the water god Ea/Enki and his faithful follower Utnapishtim, who survived the great Flood because he followed the god's wise instructions to build an ark and save as many lives as possible; as we have seen, Utnapishtim was rewarded with eternal life on the paradisial island of Dilmun. This island was a real place; today it is called Bahrain. About a hundred years after Enheduanna died, a settlement was founded on the island, which is in the Persian Gulf, and dedicated to Ea/Enki. Vegetable farming flourished, and archaeologists today believe the area was a thriving commercial center where ships stopped to load and unload cargo traded between Sumer and the coast of India. Dilmun was mythologized as a place with no illness or violence—even, in fact, with no death.

After the Sumerian culture merged into the Akkadian and then the Babylonian cultures, "paradise" came to be described as a garden, a walled-in place of perfection kept safely guarded from nature's whims of flood, disease, and drought. The word "paradise" itself stems from a Persian term for "walled-in gar-den." In some religious imaginations, paradise eventually became located somewhere off the planet in a place of unearthly per-fection. This concentration of a defined "goodness" all in one place necessitated an equal concentration of a defined "evil," located imaginatively in a torturous hell. Scholar Rita Casey de-scribed the roots of this idea as "discrete" or partial conscious-ness, one brought about through myths of the god Enki. Inan-na's grandfather was god of both water and the engineering of its flows, so crucial to farming in the river regions of Sumer. Irrigation technology, Casey has argued, led to an elevation of the fruits of human imagination, separating mind from matter. This development reflects a split in human consciousness, away from nature's paradoxical reality of combining good and bad, and into concepts that overvalue human fantasy and desire for perfection, balanced with concepts of original sin, flawed hu-manity, and even a despising of the earth as "unclean." Thus, Sumer held two differing views of life and its endings, meanings, and possibilities. The conflict is evident in Inanna's destruction of Mt. Ebih (discussed in chapter 4) *because it would not bow down to her.* Betty Meador's interpretation was that the poet Enhed-uanna embraced the immanence of contradictory sacred con-sciousness (Inanna) throughout nature and addressed the ideal of paradise as a "rebel" that Inanna's fierce changeability would inevitably destroy.

Centuries later, in a twist, the story of Gilgamesh and his warrior friend now define a brand-new worldview, one that ba-sically rejects both of the earlier ones and ultimately leads to materialism and secular humanism. This third worldview is the rejection of traditional religion and the belief in an afterlife and, more impactfully, the establishment as an ultimate "good" the drastic idea that earth is to be exploited on behalf of humanity without heed to any other life-forms. Materialist ideologies, in a quest for supporting increasing longevity, good health, and comfortable conveniences for human life, have been some of the most destructive to the matrix of all life, especially following industrialization. However, the free thinking made possible by secular humanism's skepticism also supports the endless curiosity and attempts at "objectivity" of science. Recently, scientists have added ecological responsibility and alarms about human-driven climate crises to the relentless quest to extend human life and desire for comforts.

These three worldviews of life after death—immanent reincarnation of the soul in another earthly, possibly creature, form; journey of the soul to paradise or hell; and simply materialism, with no lasting soul—overlap, influence one another, are constantly in flux, yet retain their distinct characters and implications. We live in the midst of them all and billions of people embrace, often fiercely, one or another of them. For example, Shakti as immanent and conscious energy of life survives in modern India, as does reincarnation. This belief system continues not only in most of Hinduism, but also in Buddhism, Taoism, Sikhism, some forms of Christianity, and many indigenous earth-based religions.

The paradise myth was inherited by all the Abrahamic religions, conceived as a set-aside garden, an imaginary place "in heaven," and a reward for a faith-based life. The viewpoint is optimistic, still able to imagine life after death—a soul or spirit existing somewhere, just not reborn into an earthly body. Some paradise myths predict a single event of mass resurrection and establishment of a perfect, deathless world of human beings on earth.

Secular humanism pushed away from all religion, placing its emphasis on rationality and denial of any afterlife of any kind, and also denial of consciousness in nature. Recently, the belief in human beings as the sole reservoir of consciousness has been challenged as science engages with and records the real lives of creatures, and as examples of paranormal experience accumulate. Humanistic materialism accompanies communism, and, very differently, settled into much of postwar Europe as secularism. These three viewpoints continually trade ideas and practices across the whole world, influencing one another yet retaining the essentials of their very different approaches to life, death, afterlife, and, most crucially, connection or disconnection of humans to nature. What more can Inanna's stories teach us about this?

3

O My Wild, Ecstatic Cow!

When the clay tablets the Sumerian poets left in the sand were found and translated four thousand years later, they contained some of the world's richest literature: creation stories, a Flood myth, dramatic hero journeys, even instructions for farming. The poems are teeming with interesting deities and dramatic stories. No one received more attention from the poets, apparently, than Inanna, the third brightest light in the sky, so vividly brilliant in the western firmament that you can see her eight points with the naked eye. Small wonder that in the imaginations of the ancient Sumerians, when she dipped low on the horizon she easily stepped onto the earth, sat next to people in the tavern, hung out with horses in the stable, and avidly took part in human affairs. She was a consummate shapeshifter, and her poets and artists used many different images to describe her, including lion, bird, snake, dragon, beloved of the Sky god, receiver of cosmic powers, sovereign lady of blazing dominion, queen of heaven and earth. My favorite passionate name for Inanna, written well over four thousand years ago, is the poet Enheduanna calling out to her: "O my wild, ecstatic cow!" What made the goddess Inanna wild and ecstatic, as well as having blazing dominion? She is a combination of human, creature, erotic and other energetic forces, and civilization. She also inherited very old powers that grew out of women's rituals.

What Is This Blood?

The myth of Inanna and Shukaletuda relates that in her zeal to confront the errant gardener and bring him to justice,

Inanna forces her grandfather Enki to pay attention to the seriousness of her quest by flooding the land with blood. What is this blood? There is no reason to suppose it was formed through violence, and there are obvious clues for my claim that this was Inanna's own blood, her powerful menses—a substance that would have held extreme positive or negative energies, depending on her intentions. Other clues include that she followed this up with a storm flood, a capacity that was credited to menstruating women (including maidens at menarche) all over the earth. The energies associated with menstruating gave indigenous women power over the weather, especially rain and wind, and in many cultures this belief held into the nineteenth century, and even still today. (In fact, only in the last few decades have weather bureaus started naming hurricanes with some male names, rather than only female names.)

Inanna sought to gain the attention of her Sumerian people and the gods who were in charge of natural forces, and she had dramatic methods. When the undrinkable blood pouring out of wells and rivers didn't gain her what she wanted, and the fierce storm with flooding didn't help her either, her final blow was to block up the roads, stopping all travel, escape, and commerce. This too is related to worldwide menstrual powers, as women on their periods were typically prohibited from traveling, and this prohibition applied to the men in their lives as well. In many cultures, men did not go hunting or traveling when their wives were in seclusion with their periods.

India provides an instructive example. In its agrarian cultures similar to that of ancient Sumer, the south Indian goddess Bhumi Devi, who was the earth itself, menstruated every year. During her annual period, the entire society shut down for three days. No one worked, debts were erased, and on her emergence people celebrated. This custom ceased about a century ago, but in the northeastern Indian state of Assam, the earth goddess Kamakhya continues to menstruate, proof of which is a red color appearing occasionally in the nearby river.

My own research in south India in the 1990s showed correlations between menstrual customs in various communities and the rituals of the temple goddesses Bhadrakali, Bhagavathi, Parvati, and Mariamma. Maidens were and are goddesses during their numinous initiations, and conversely goddess rituals were modeled after home menstrual practices. Deep connections exist between human development of ideas of deity, spirit, creation figures—and women's blood powers.

The names of at least two ancient Greek goddesses reflect this close connection, especially to the vulva. Pallas Athena literally means "womb womb"; Hera is also "womb." The Romans so revered the planet Venus as one of their esteemed goddesses, they coined the word "veneration" as adoration of her. Later as religious authority opposed Venus's open sexuality, she picked up "venereal" and "venial" as well, but essentially "Venus" means "desire" and "fulfillment." Even in contemporary times, physiologists named the mound overlooking the vulva for the bright planet goddess, "mons veneris" meaning "mountain of Venus."

While mainstream mass culture does not recognize a connection between menstruation and electromagnetism, earlier and less materialist peoples used this idea as a central organizing principle. Ancestral groups all over the world prescribed rules for a young girl's first period, as well as for women's monthly periods thereafter, in terms of bioelectrical energies and other subtle energy forms of nature. Frequently they used a binary model similar to what our materialist industrial world uses for electricity—a positive (conductive) and negative (insular) charge. They applied this to subtle streams of bioenergy. These streams were understood as chaotic when our bodies are too open—for example, when menstruating, giving birth, in an altered state of consciousness, or in an emotionally vulnerable state. Therefore, people applied measures to bring these energies under control so no one would be harmed. This is the principal idea behind prohibiting menstruating women from participating in rituals such as sweat lodge, temple rites, and many other public gatherings. Parallel to this is the reaction that men's bodies can have to menstruating women, distracting them from their own rites. The protections were put in place for participants, for the menstruating woman, and for the effectiveness of the rituals. As cultures convert to materialism, they drop or change the meanings of these customs.

Maidens at menarche the world over were fed insulating foods (simple cooked grains) and prohibited from conductive foods—especially meat (blood) and salt. Maidens' bodies might also be cloaked in insulating materials such as plant fibers or wood products used as capes or hoods; in a girl's highly charged state, her body might be separated from earth by wood, including prototypes of shoes (wood blocks, coconut shells) and cloth (sitting on a mat, walking on cloth, wrapped in a simple cloth).

When her bleeding was finished, she was ritually bathed and dressed. Her clothing and jewelry served to protect her body from unwanted energetic influences. According to my electrical adviser, conductive metal jewelry—copper, silver, gold—extends our own bioelectric circuits and makes them less chaotic and intense. Conversely, insulating metal, cloth, plant fibers, and wood prevent other people's energies from interfering with ours.

There is little understanding of this in mainstream culture, which has left any notion of bioelectrical emanations far behind; therefore, certain practices of indigenous peoples have been misconstrued. For instance, terms for a woman's menstrual state were mistranslated as "pollution." A better term would be "overcharged" or even "amped up" in an electromagnetic sense. Ancient peoples sought to protect themselves, and especially young initiates, from hot charges or chaotic energies. The life force was frequently deified and understood as conscious and approachable.

Earth mother or goddess science usually revolves around concepts of hot and cold—high charges of energy and cooling agents to calm the charges so they are not harmful. Trying to keep the goddess (the life force) heated enough to be animating, but not so hot as to cause tumult, is a primary goal of many rituals. When the goddess is upright, naked, and dancing, she is more excited and also more dangerous; when she is fully robed and standing or seated, she is calmed and approachable. Sumerian poetry describes the ritual weeping of priests and priestesses as being for the purpose of cooling the goddess down during troubled times. One of her poet-priestesses wrote, of her own grief: "Flow tears / cooling drink for Inanna."

When I visited south India in the 1990s, goddess temples and rituals were everywhere. People freely and proudly told me about the feasts, processions, and rituals their families had used to initiate daughters at menarche. The rituals of the goddess in temple installations were similar to those of the initiated maidens, and in some communities, the maiden was said to embody the goddess when she emerged from her menstrual seclusion, was ritually bathed, and was dressed in finery. Communities that could afford it gave their daughters elaborate processions and feasts.

In south India I found that the elements of first menstruation had been these: show of blood drops, seclusion for set number of days of the maiden, emergence as a rebirth, ritual bathing and oiling, dressing her in finery and honoring her with a public procession, noisy, joyful, full of music. The rites for the maidens in various communities also overlap with rites for goddesses. Historically for many families, the maiden embodied a goddess during her menarche rites.

As her poetry reveals, these elements are all part of the rituals of goddess Inanna. And this sequence of events seems to have become a major mythic story, "The Descent of Inanna into the Underworld." When the goddess is stripped down to nakedness and struck by her elder sister before she undergoes a ritual three-day death, followed by resurrection and emergence with new powers, Inanna's descent myth replicates the seclusion of the maiden at menarche. In some Middle Eastern and eastern European families, the mother strikes her daughter across the face on learning she has begun menstruating for the first time. The women I have spoken to about this do not know why this custom persists; it's just a gesture handed down over the generations. At the very least it shocks the girl into paying attention. Other correlations with menarche include a prohibition about eating in the below-world, and another forbidding any men from going near the maiden in her rituals. In the myth, no male gods were willing to visit the underworld; it was cross-gendered characters, presumably freed from gendered taboos, who effected Inanna's resurrection.

Processions for Honoring Inanna

A goddess, most typically, is a composite of women's collective rituals, plus aspects of nature. Inanna is a goddess with distinct cycles; she has her own orbit as a planet whirling around the sun, and is the closest planet to our own orbit. Her priests and priestesses also marked a lunar cycle for her, which means she was understood as a menstrual being. This was a source of her power. Every month at the new moon, the gods gathered around her to protect the *mes*, the functional laws that she had received. She sat with An, the Sky god, on the dais in the heavens; she determined the fates of the land with Enlil, the Wind god. She decreed judgments; she decided verdicts along with Enlil. Her people paraded before her.

As the planet Inanna rose in the evening, a "great torch in the evening sky," her people marched by in front of her. The procession was noisy and sensual, with singing and drumming on four kinds of drums, each rousing a different kind of internal state. Bold smells filled the air; "incense offerings like a forest of aromatic cedars [were] transmitted to her." The earth was sanctified. From her position in the western sky, the brilliant goddess looked down upon the procession with joy; she was "the lady of the evening."

This lively procession was led by male prostitutes who had tied up their hair and were wearing colorful scarves. They were followed by righteous men and women carrying harps of peacefulness. The men dressed half in men's clothing, half in women's. The women dressed half in men's clothing, half in women's, and using colorful jump ropes, competed in greeting Inanna. Warriors passed by, lifting their swords to salute her. The *kurgarru* priests did their particular dance with curved swords, and drummers in groups offered their rhythms to greet Inanna in the sky. Certain priests carried swords dripping with some kind of blood, probably animal or bird sacrifice, or even their own; they spattered the drops as they walked. Blood was also poured on the throne seat—as though to energize it for the goddess. Young men walked in procession with neck yokes on their shoulders.

Some of the details of this Sumerian description struck me because I have witnessed similar offerings in Kerala. For instance, jumping rope, like an agrarian ritual of women swinging in north India, may indicate that young women were charged with helping the plants grow high.

The south Indian goddess Bhadrakali has shamans who dance with swords in similar fashion to descriptions of the *kurgarru* priests who danced for Inanna. These Indian shamans, veli-chapads, sing songs to arouse the sexual energies of the goddess, and they go into trance states by making their own heads bleed.

I was reminded of the young men in neck yokes during Sumerian times one day when I witnessed a ritual dance of Kavady in a south Indian village. In this ritual, young men danced down a road for hours while bearing heavy, thick wooden yokes, used in the past to carry pails of water for the bath of the goddess. With this burden bearing, they were exhibiting their complete devotion to the goddess, and their surrender to her as her "captives."

I'm guessing that the Sumerian poet-storytellers, steeped for generations in practices of puberty seclusions that equated with visiting the womb of creation and being reborn, wrote their stories in a larger context, with a single deity representing "women" and more broadly everyone, and a plot of death and resurrection pertaining to all civic and natural life. Heroes went on journeys to slay dragons or locate the secret to eternal life. In perhaps an "annual menstruation," the goddess Inanna went on a descent journey into the womb of the earth, the below-world that, following her resurrection, gave her powers to command life, death, and judgment over rebirth. She used this Eye of Death in rendering the fate of her lover Dumuzi, as well as Shukaletuda, the errant gardener—setting his fate that he could not be reborn.

Love and Erotic Power in a Living World

The Sumerian poets reflected a quirky sensibility of people deeply in touch with the lively, animated world, able to see from a variety of points of view, and with a sense of humor. For instance, one poem is a rivalry-insult dialogue, "The debate between Grain and Sheep."

Grain says, "Sister, I am your better. I take precedence over you. I am the glory of the lights of the Land." Grain brags further, "I am the gift of the old gods . . . when I confer my power on the warrior he goes to war knowing no fear."

Sheep replies, rather sarcastically, "You, like holy Inanna . . . love horses." (And not sheep, obviously.) However, Sheep goes on to demolish Grain's proud bearing with these words (I'm paraphrasing):

"But on the threshing floor, even a lowly captured enemy, held by a rope, pounds the pestle into your face, crushes your mouth and ears; the north and south wind blow you all around, and the pestle and mortar make your body into flour."

The Sumerian language was written in two different dialects; one of these was Emesal, a specialized "women's language" used in writing love poetry, hymns, and proverbs, especially when the voice of a goddess or woman is speaking in the poem. This was a spoken language as well, and one of Inanna's entertainments was "to see that women amuse themselves by speaking children's language, to see that children amuse themselves by using women's language." Emesal was also the dialect of choice for a poem in which a cow is speaking, and again when a temple wall is speaking.

Love poems about Inanna's passion, for which she is rightly renowned, would have been written in Emesal, and this suggests they were composed by women. The poems celebrate women's bodies, feelings, and sexuality:

She leaned back against the apple tree.
When she leaned against the apple tree,

her vulva was wondrous to behold.
Rejoicing at her wondrous vulva,
the young woman Inanna applauded herself.

This next poem, translated by Betty Meador, gives us some sense of what that wonder was about:

where I'm coming from
my vulva is
the power place . . .
I rule with cunt power
I see with cunt eyes . . .
This is where
I'm coming from . . .
With my vulva
I live right here
in this soft slit
I live right here

The celebration of her vulva had made me wonder whether Inanna was ever portrayed with a clitoris. My puzzlement increased after I found a photo online of a bas-relief of Ishtar lying naked and flat on her marriage bed, with a pubic triangle outline in the clay, and at the narrow end between her thighs an unmistakable little evocative knob.

Inanna is the goddess who allows public sexual intercourse in her sanctuary, the Kulaba. Inanna's love poems are from a woman's point of view, and although her lavish descriptions of her beloved are totally connected to the agrarian economy for which she was responsible, preparations for lovemaking are carefully done. Inanna describes how she bathes and oils her body, asks her mother to make up a love bed and sprinkle cedar oil on it, in anticipation of lovemaking with the shepherd king and bull god Dumuzi.

As said earlier, Inanna's own pleasure is absolutely necessary, and her lovemaking is intricately involved in the abundance of field, orchard, meadow, forest, and joy of heart in the people.

> My eager impetuous caresser of the navel,
> My caresser of the soft thighs,
> He is the one my womb loves best,
> He is lettuce planted by the water.

In other Sumerian poetry the goddess herself is compared to an ibex (a mountain goat with impossibly long slender brown horns arcing over its back). She is compared to a red deer. She is offered butter: "Lady, going to the sweet-voiced cows and gentle-voiced calves in the cattle-pen, young woman, when you arrive there, may the churn sound! May the churn of your spouse sound, Inanna, may the churn sound!"

The Sumerian poets used irony and humor, as in one poem of a young man telling his equally young lover, Inanna, how to fool her mother in order to be with him:

> let me tell you what to say
> let me tell you what to say
> let me tell you women's lies, sweet Inanna
> say
> my girlfriend took me to the square
> we danced to the tambourine
> she sang her mournful songs
>   and I listened
> she sang her joyous songs
>   and I listened

time slipped away
tell your Divine mother this lie
say really! it is true! . . .
then we will watch the moon cross the sky
come lie in the bed I will spread for you
come lie in my pure untouched bed
we have the whole night
      hours of sweet time!

Hours of sweet time to pleasure them both—as I have said, Inanna insisted that she be pleased sensually and sexually, the kind of eroticism that produces prolonged states of ecstasy and releases joy into the world.

Inanna's woman friend and warrior pal, the shamanic, virginal, protective goddess-queen Ninshubur, plays multiple roles of lamentation, rescue, and fighting, and her own poem calls her independent and "flying" in ecstatic joy. These qualities place her solidly in a column of artful lesbianism, even warrior dyke. The two females are also emotionally entangled, since Ninshubur goes to great trouble to effect Inanna's rescue from the underworld, and Inanna in turn rescues Ninshubur with a passionate speech about her faithfulness when demons are mistakenly trying to drag the shaman into the underworld.

In one of the courtship poems about the sacred marriage of Inanna and Dumuzi, Ninshubur serves also as a kind of elevated bridesmaid, leading the beloved new husband to Inanna's "sweet thighs" in her marriage bed and making it clear that it is Inanna who will provide him with his powers, and the abundance that will follow is an abundance throughout the whole land. In return, as the "shepherd king," he is to protect everything and keep it fertile; however, the poetry makes clear that the source of the grain and vegetation is from the female: "May the Lady of Vegetation pile the grain in heaps and mounds."

In a different poem, Inanna claims the farming arts:

I poured out plants from my womb . . .
I poured out grain from my womb.

Ninshubur blesses the couple:

My queen, here is the choice of your heart,
the king, your beloved bridegroom.
May he spend long days in the sweetness of your holy loins.
Give him a favorable and glorious reign.

Even aside from raising earth energy to feed plants and animals, the capacity to go into a light trance—during sex or some other trance-inducing activity—seems to open the body as an extended mind, allowing images and beautiful senses that are connective and expansive at the same time.

Regulating All That Energy: Amulets and Implements

From the fact that Inanna's temple at Uruk featured a sanctuary where public sexual intercourse was encouraged—and that the poets wrote such erotic poetry to her—it seems that Sumerian society, at least in some periods, encouraged much shamanic presence and erotic play, while at the same time requiring the grounded discipline of craftspeople, farmers, traders, and so on. As a passionate people with high emotions, Sumerians would need to regulate all that energetic or electromagnetic activity in some way. Drumming and singing would help balance some of it, and processions were full of this music and dance. Archaeologists unearthing personal goods of Sumerians have found astonishing amounts of finely made jewelry, the oldest of which was made around 2700 BCE.

The Sumerians excelled in the making of jewelry, much of which served as protective amulets directly on their bodies. Everyone—not just the elite groups in the temples and palaces—draped themselves in anklets, rings, necklaces, earrings, and so on. Women wore the most jewelry. I am struck by the similarity of my experience in south India, where all traditional women wear anklets, bracelets, and earrings—gold if they can afford it, otherwise silver. These are for protection as well as being attractive and valuable. Once, when I was staying overnight at a farmhouse near the Malabar Coast, one of the older household members rubbed her hands along my arms in obvious alarm and insisted I go to the nearby festival grounds and get myself some bracelets "to protect your arms."

How this protection might work is that, as I said, bioenergies are electromagnetic, traveling in currents or emanations. A ring of conductive metal (such as copper, silver, or gold) extends one's own current and reduces its intensity. An Indian friend told me that small items made of iron are used by women in her generation as a conductive safeguard; she carries an iron key in her purse when she is on her period. Another Indian friend wrote that even the goddess could have "too much Shakti," and that a woman coming out of seclusion after her period, even bathed and dressed to interact with her family, might carry too much energy; she would need to eat something to ground herself further before seeing her children. So the energy is only negative when it is too intense and disruptive.

Amulets are usually shiny. They work by diverting "the evil eye"—other people's eye emanations—in order to prevent them from negatively affecting you. The idea is that the amulet catches the first glance, which is presumed to be the most potent. The feeling behind the glance is believed to be an unconscious beam of envy. Sumerians also protected against "demons," or energetic forces believed to cause disease and misfortune. One such force was the lilitu, later associated with Lilith.

Besides jewelry, which I am more tempted to think of as "implements," the way a goddess (or god) dresses and stands indicates the state of power they are in. Calling all this worked stone and metal "decorations" or "ornaments" seems short of the point—they are also more than signifiers. Each piece serves a function—for instance, of protection, of diversion, of conduction, and of imparting a sense of well-being and responsible bearing.

Inanna herself dresses in a variety of stunning outfits. One poem describes her choosing a string of beads for her buttocks, a ring for her navel, a lapis necklace for her neck, ribbons of gold over the tops of her ears and bronze earrings in her lobes, "head stones" across her forehead, honey lotion for her face and hips, strands of shining alabaster around her thighs, black willow wood to cover her vulva, something made of gold shaped like "genitals" to put in her hair, and ornate sandals "on her toes."

In one depiction, the goddess wears a robe dress pleated in such a way as to resemble levels of a ziggurat, a temple with terraces each smaller than the one below; this robe has a split up the side, and one muscled, slender bare leg protrudes, bent at the knee, foot resting on a crouching lion. Rain arrows or lightning bolts shoot from Inanna's shoulders, and on her head she wears the triple crown of the steppe: three sets of bull horns, one on top of the other. She is dressed as though to depict the known cosmos—sky above with crescent horns, then mountain, then her sandals, which, as one poem says, are the flat earth itself. The naked-leg pose would be perfectly at home in a Las Vegas chorus line or at a strip club as a provocative, sexually enticing gesture. However, Inanna's grandfather Enki also dresses in a pleated robe with one naked leg stuck out proactively. Everything the Sumerians did seemed to tie them to their cosmos and the stories they told about the nature of reality, and with meanings we can only guess.

Another illustration, one of my favorites, shows Inanna naked except for her horned crown; she holds a measuring line and rod, ready for action—perhaps even prepared to cause some changes in the weather. She dresses for her differing powers— here she is a rainmaker, nude and full of lightning; elsewhere she is an observing bird, again naked but with bird feet; in her full pleated robe, she is standing calmly to receive libations and offerings of sheep, grain, birds, fish, butter, and semiprecious stones. Seated she is robed and cool, logical, an administrator doling out categories and chores, "fixing fates," as her poets say. Naked she is heated, whipping up energies—of sex, of weather, of plant growth, of battle. Her poetry describes her dressing to go to battle, with a "young man's visage," with a mace or arrow. Battle, the poets tell us, is "Inanna's dance."

Inanna's Tools or Weapons

Poems, songs, and stories about Inanna tie her character to themes of love, sexuality, civic life, nature, and justice. Another side of Inanna is connected to war, battle, ferocity. She has a full range of powers. The word "battle" appears as often in her poetry as do the words "love," "lovely," and "beloved."

But often "battle" is paired with "storm" or "storm-wind"; it's as though the warriors mentioned in the poems were exhorted to have the strength and courage of a storm—of Inanna *as* a storm. Battle is her dance, and she sets up conflicts; she herself holds a variety of military weapons—arrow, quiver, bow, mace, spear. She has capacity "to subdue the hostile enemy." Soldiers called on her to assist them; she was also protector of Sargon I, who founded the Akkadian dynasty and became the first known emperor. In the 2300s BCE, he established an empire that covered all Mesopotamia and beyond, from the Zagros Mountains in the east to the cedar forests at the Mediterranean shore. He sent ships to India for trade.

Sargon was born of a priestess who could not keep him; she put him in a reed basket on the river, and he was adopted by a gardener. He rose high in the kingdom, becoming the cupbearer of King Ur-Zababa of Kish, a position that may have been second in command because so much trust was involved, given the king's enemies would try to poison him. The cupbearer may also have interpreted his own and the king's dreams, as a kind of divination. That is what happened when Sargon dreamed that Inanna had drowned the king in blood. On hearing this Ur-Zababa became extremely paranoid; he told a goldsmith at the royal foundry that he would send Sargon with a golden mirror, and the smith must throw them both into the blazing cauldron. Sargon was steps away from the door to the foundry when Inanna intercepted him and blocked his way. "You can't go in there," she said. "No one who is polluted with blood can enter the foundry."

Why would Sargon be considered under a blood taboo? He wasn't yet a warrior; he was responsible for serving cups of wine in the palace. *That* may be the connection, that wine— possibly being socially constructed as "menstrual blood of the earth"—was kept separated from the arts of metallurgy, and especially from pots of red-hot molten metal, by a "blood taboo" of the goddesses. Or I would even say that Sargon's dream of blood might have put him into a "polluted state." In any case, the separation of electromagnetic states was in effect. Clearly blood and its taboos are another of Inanna's powers— or weapons.

"Weapon" can mean a method of gaining an advantage. It's in this sense that I understand the weapons of the goddesses of India who resemble Inanna and vice versa. Their multiple sets of hands hold what are called "weapons," which can include: a lotus, a lamp, a conch (which makes the sound "aum"), a bell, a cobra, a mirror, a scythe, a hammer to break up stone—in addition to what English speakers consider "weapons": sword, arrow, knife. I'm thinking Inanna's eight-pointed rosette symbol could be related to the north Indian lotus, which has eight petals as its base, and the meaning of "creatrix, a general term for many different goddesses." On my wall at home, a poster of the Indian goddess Bhadrakali shows her wearing an amulet design of a flower with eight buds; it's identical to one of Inanna's symbols. As I have said, the two areas, India and Sumer, were tied together through trade and cultural exchange, especially by sea, and possibly also through migration from the Zagros Mountains that border the Tigris-Euphrates valley to the Indus Valley civilization.

Although Inanna possessed arrows and quiver, as well as the arts of the hero passed to her when she was given the cosmic powers, most of Inanna's weapons seem to have been quite benign. Included in these *mes* were the tools of the craftspeople, brickmakers and weavers, and measuring lines for laying out temples and palaces. And I would also add as her tools the cart, and the tavern.

Inanna's Cart

While the cart may have begun as a two-wheeled vehicle for hauling a goddess icon to a high place to greet the moon, it became the chariot of war, and the reason for building roads. It also has an intriguing connection to LGBT slang.

As I have said, the religion of Inanna and other Sumerian deities involved elaborate processions that included cross-dressed people, cross-gender people, and colorful priestly garb. Inanna was depicted in cylinder seals sitting on a throne, standing with wings on lions, standing on winged harnessed lions, and standing on the axle between winged lions pulling a cart. Her characteristics spread wherever farming arts did: when the practices surrounding her and similar goddesses spread out from Sumer into the rest of the Middle East, the Mediterranean, and central Europe, images of goddesses riding in carts persisted through the ages. For example, winged Nike rode in a chariot pulled by horses; the Roman goddess Cybele rode in splendor in a cart pulled by lions; and statues of Roman "winged Victory" in a cart are widespread across many countries.

Inanna riding in a cart has also echoed through centuries of European folk customs. Processions featured beautifully dressed young women and transvestism, the latter including men dressed as queens and people of both sexes wearing leather and horns like the horned god. The Fool's King New Year festivals of Spain, Italy, France, and England, with drunken revelry, nudity, lewdness, mocking of authorities, and cross-dressed people pulling or riding in carts (floats), preceded today's raucous Halloween processions, Mardi Gras, and other festive occasions. The antiquated word for "cart" in English is "drag." To be "in drag" became tied to cross-dressing and being outrageously expressive. "Drag queens" and "drag kings" seem to be related to old pagan customs of gods and goddesses riding in a cart in public display.

And that brings me to the origins of the term "drag" as pertaining to cross-dressing men, on ceremonial occasions such as parade floats and onstage. In my youth in the early 1960s, I first met drag queens in underground, and rather dangerous, bars. Later, Gay Pride and Halloween processions and street festivals allowed very free expression of cross-dressing.

In my experience, drag queens were not imitating women; they were dressing as queens. That's why they were not called "drag women." Actually, drag queens were dressing in forms of women's power. It's as though they were projecting what looks powerfully "feminine" to them onto a screen in their minds, and imitating that. Often this projection is part of the overall social projection of glamour embodied by such popular stars as Lady Gaga, Beyoncé, and Marilyn Monroe.

Many feminists of the 1970s misunderstood this, probably because everyone had been taught for so long that nearly everything of any substance in any society was a product of male efforts and imaginations. Even by 1980, U.S. women did not yet have access to enough historical and anthropological information to counter this ideology. This is why cultural feminists (such as myself) became "women-centered"—to try to rebalance the story, as women in the West developed into a political position the belief that men so control women that men somehow began at some point to force women to wear whatever would make them constricted, masked, and physically weak. For a few years, feminists dressed as warriors, thinking that plain clothing and flat shoes brought protection to women from unwanted sexist attention. Women, specifically "lipstick lesbians," who countered this idea by dressing in heels and as much makeup as they wished, created a schism in the movement, even triggering pickets of protest over a "lipstick lesbian" on the cover of an Olivia Records album, around 1978. (This is not to deny that some men do co-opt, manipulate, mock, and exploit women's clothing, hairstyles, gestures, and so on). Nevertheless the high heels, makeup, earrings, hairdos, sexy dresses, and postures are original to women's own invention. (I understand that this is an oversimplification, but I think the point is valuable.)

Not until spiritual feminism arose did ideas of women's beauty as a development by and for women surface. My own work, especially 1993's *Blood, Bread, and Roses*, contributed research on origins of high heels, lipstick, earrings, and so forth, as part of women's powers in describing human knowledge.

In the meantime, feminists very vocally accused drag queens of making fun of women, and for a while, drag virtually disappeared or went underground. Pressed by other social forces to be more masculine, gay men adopted mustaches in the mid-1970s; "drag," like "gay," became negative pop slang.

The projection of women's beauty as an element of power and expression is not only an aspect of "queens"—who must project power in order to maintain public faith in themselves as rulers—but also of goddesses. In ancient times through to modern ones, goddesses have carried this kind of beauty-power. Think of Oshun, the Yoruba goddess of love and beauty, who dresses lavishly in brilliant golden cloth and carries a hand mirror, or of Aphrodite, with her flowing hair and robes and graceful, youthful gestures. In a sense, the gay (I assumed they were gay, though who knows?) drag queens of my experience were not emulating women so much as they were projecting women's sexually attractive goddess-power, some form of the beauty of Venus, and engaging it for themselves. Now drag is back, more dramatically than ever; anyone can do it. Drag is a kind of performance art, and it's all over the world.

Inanna's Tavern

Besides honey cakes, the Sumerians used grain for beer making. Inanna is one of the goddesses credited with grain growing. She also was in charge of the sacred tavern—her priestess made her a special bed in the tavern itself—as part of her sexual rites. Many cultures have used beer drinking ritually, especially as an act of divination and a way of determining how one really feels about something. It's long been part of coming-of-age ceremonies, from the products of alewives of Africa to the pulque fermenters of central Mexico. My own European-descended uncle gave me whiskey on my coming of age, and my Scandinavian-born father used alcohol as a social leveler—if you wouldn't have a drink with him, he thought you a snob.

An interesting new study links moderate drinking with democratic countries, the author speculating that mild social drinking allows women to have greater choice in the matter of companions and sexual partners, and that women's participation in public culture leads to more prosperity and a greater degree of democracy. This openness diminishes in regions and families who engage in heavy drinking, yet even there, democracy is more present than it is in parts of the world where drinking is prohibited. Ancient Mesopotamia had primitive forms of democracy; the gods made choices and people had some influence over how they were governed. Women in the first thousand years of Sumer had more rights than in later militarized and increasingly patriarchal times. As mentioned earlier, women could own property, and they engaged in public life as business owners with their husbands; they could also be scribes, priestesses, physicians, poets, and serve as judges and witnesses. The lively productive goddesses in the Sumerian pantheon served as role models for humans, something that movie stars and other high-profile women do for society today. Choice and decision, engaging in love and sexual pleasure, and holding power are part of Inanna's inheritance of principles of the cosmos.

Ancient Mesopotamian poets described Inanna's tavern visits as associated with her divine decisions, prophecy, emotional expression, conviviality, sexuality, and inclusion. One poet had her express high emotion: "As I spin around the lake of beer, while feeling wonderful, feeling wonderful, while drinking beer, in a blissful mood . . . with joy in the heart and a contented liver—my heart is a heart filled with joy!"

4

The Woman Who Would Be Job

A Portrait of Inanna

On the wall in my bedroom there lives a sizable contemporary portrait of Inanna. She's not the slender, budlike goddess in Sumerian illustrations, naked except for a crown of horns and standing on two lions or standing in a cart with lightning coming out of her shoulders. Rather, she is shaped like the full moon, an Ishtar figure, voluptuous with a thick, round body. The background is luscious, burnt sienna, while the figure has some of that color, washed over with a silvery light. The artist, Tricia Grame, used symbols from seven-thousand-year-old goddess figures, chevrons at her neck and black cross-hatching, like thigh-high stockings, on her legs.

The portrait of Inanna is nothing if not sexy. She is holding her breasts, offering them as love and vitality, abundance and acceptance, a typical Inanna gesture. Her nipples are ringed with the spirals of the galaxies. In the middle of her dress is a sculptural effect using folded paper that forms a startling, possibly vaginal opening, provocatively set just off her actual vulva, which is only subtly suggested. The opening entices to a mysterious dark channel, almost its own underworld. Or not—maybe it's just a fold in the dress. Her head is done in black paint that resembles a charcoal drawing, and her serious face is that of the artist. Meditating on this image gives me a sense of being in touch with all the people who have adored this deity. So I know Inanna three ways: through poets, through artisans who formed her images, and through her sparkling light in the night or early morning sky.

As a child I was considered "the religious one" in a troubled family and given a handsome Bible. One of my favorite and most valued sections was the Book of Job, a story addressing suffering and how to get yourself through it. After I grew up, life became even harder, though also with high times, as I discovered foreign movies, theatrical art, and great music. My attention went to *J.B.*, a play about Job written by the poet Archibald MacLeish. At age twenty-five, I fell into a coma and was not expected to live. When I awoke, I had lost temporarily my ability to speak coherently. I could sing, however, and the song was a happy one, sung by children, and from the play *J.B.* My life changed, and I was on what felt like my "true path." Whatever happened to me during my unconscious time, it involved the story of Job.

Twenty years later a student came to work with me who later became a friend and colleague: Betty De Shong Meador, a Jungian analyst who said she needed a teacher "who could work with the dark." She was transfixed by the writing of a woman poet named Enheduanna, of whom I had never heard. Betty collaborated closely with a Sumerian scholar and brought to my class line upon line of this ancient poet, rendered skillfully into contemporary poetry. Some of it was gorgeous and lyrical, and some of it was startlingly violent. I saw what Betty meant by "the dark."

I too became transfixed with this work and with the story in it. As with Job, the poetry seemed to teach how to endure suffering in one's life, how to get through the emotional devastation of feeling innocent yet losing everything. Unlike the biblical story, the Sumerian poet was addressing her grievances not to a god but rather to a goddess, Inanna, who also happened to be that sparkling light in the early night sky that has attracted me all my life; as a child I began speaking to it (when no one was looking). To be introduced to marvelous poetry dedicated to her completely enthralled me.

The Book of Job and the Poetry of Enheduanna

Both the Book of Job and the poetry of Enheduanna have informed my life. They also have caught my poet's heart with the grandeur of their poetry. Here is Job, speaking of God in the King James Version:

> *But he knoweth the way that I take: when he hath tried me, I shall come forth as gold.*
> *My foot hath held his steps, his way have I kept, and not declined.*
> *Neither have I gone back from the commandment of his lips; I have esteemed the words of his mouth more than my necessary food.*
> *But he is in one mind, and who can turn him? and what his soul desireth, even that he doeth.*

And here is Enheduanna describing her goddess, in Betty Meador's translation:

> steps, yes she steps her narrow foot
> on the furred back
> of a wild lapis lazuli bull
>
> and she goes out
> white-sparked, radiant
> in the dark vault of evening's sky
> star-steps in the street
> through the Gate of Wonder . . .
>
> Lady of largest heart . . .
> eldest daughter of the Moon
> in all lands supreme
> tower among great rulers . . .

what your hands have made
cannot be shoved away . . .

your "so be it"
is a final "so be it" . . .

in your dwelling
the great gods stand
saying sweet prayers

and praise
your dreadful brilliance
gladly live
at your lofty breast

Enheduanna, the earliest poet whose name we know, was
high priestess of the moon temple at Ur; she lived from 2285–
2250 BCE. She was a prominent and pious woman, holding the
highest theological office in her land of Sumer. She was a poet
who used her art to elevate the goddess Inanna, and also to tell
her own personal story of having been overthrown and exiled.
Enduring social and physical suffering, she stayed in intense
and complicated dialogue with her deity, praising and describing
her powers, entreating her assistance, and asking the goddess to
"cool her heart"—until her ordeal finally ended, and the priestess was restored to her high position in the temple.

Enheduanna was the daughter of the Akkadian king Sargon
I; scholars believe her mother was Sumerian. The poets of this
land inherited a recent invention of writing, using a wooden stylus to make marks in tiny tablets of clay. This writing, called
cuneiform, amazingly lasted 3500 years buried in sand after the
collapse of Sumer. Archaeologists uncovered the clay treasures

in the middle of the eighteenth century, and scholars began the task of translating them, making them available ever since, a great gift to literature.

At one point, while translating the Sumerian poet-priestess, Betty said, "This reads like an autobiography of real events. It's like a diary." Near the end of her translations, she said, "This is like Job!" I thought about this, took a look at the Bible, and agreed; however, we didn't have time to explore this further. Now I want to compare the two stories, using my poet's lens, to see if it seems likely that Enheduanna's work is the core story of Job. This earlier authorship may become visible by examining the historic circumstances and comparing the plots, emotions, words and phrases, and lessons of each work.

Given that the course of a life is likely full of bumpy curves and switchbacks, nearly everyone has had at least one crisis of despair, a time that seems to rob life of its central meaning. At some point nearly everyone wonders, why go on? The story of how to continue in such circumstances, one that has given understanding and comfort to hundreds of millions of people in the Abrahamic traditions, is central to the Book of Job. The story of Job (known in Hebrew as Iyov) was included in the Tanakh collection, later than the Torah and other books. Scholars think it was placed in the "Writings" section of the Tanakh as late as 400 BCE. Job is known as the prophet Ayoub in the Koran, and a much shorter version of his story is told there too.

Job was a prominent and pious man when Satan, a supernatural character, whispered in God's ear and persuaded him to "test Job's faith" by tormenting him. God took away Job's wealth, his land and livestock, and then even his children. Job still remained in a state of faith in the midst of his shock. Satan again whispered in God's ear, "But put forth thine hand now, and touch his bone and his flesh, and he will curse thee to thy face."

Satan, with God's permission, gave Job physical torments as well as social outcast status, taking away his position in the community. Job moved beyond grief into anger and began to argue, leading eventually to one of the best dramatic sequences in the Bible, the one beginning, "Where wast thou when I laid the foundations of the earth? . . . who laid the corner stone thereof; when the morning stars sang together, and all the sons of God shouted for joy?" This lengthy list led Job to a state of humility; he stopped taking his suffering so personally, and this action healed him. Job and God reconciled.

Through years of study, and doing the comparisons in this chapter, I believe that Enheduanna framed the original poetic story (which became Job's story) around her own suffering, and her love, devotion to, and exaltation of Inanna.

Here is the case that Enheduanna's poetry became the central poetic drama of the Book of Job.

How Enheduanna's Story Became Job's Story

The poet of Inanna whose identity is known, as I've said, served as a high priestess in the city of Ur at Sumer. Her name, pronounced "En-hedu-an-na," literally means "high priestess ornament of heaven." She held the highest religious office in that theocratic land. By definition she was the most righteous and faithful of persons, and she also tells us this. Her writing of her own suffering appears to be autobiographical, and she signed her work. In addition, a portrait of her, with her name on the back, was found in the ruins of Ur, where she lived, ruled, and wrote nearly four thousand years ago.

In contrast, the poet or multiple writers who wrote the central story of Job is unknown by scholars, nor is it known whether

Job was a real person or a character in a fable. The Book of Job, with its forty-one chapters, appears to be a compilation by more than one author, with central poetry telling the essential story, surrounded by extensive prose dialogues—arguments between Job and his friends—that detail some of the theological issues. The four men sit with him ostensibly to give him solace in his great misery. However, the point of their discussions is to persuade him to admit that he must have committed some sin or this tragedy would not have happened. God rewards the righteous and punishes the wicked, they insist. Job does not agree.

The Job book was incorporated into Jewish theological writing about four hundred years before the birth of Jesus, but is believed to be much older than this. Speculations range from the possibilities that Job might have lived in the time of Abraham, Moses, or Esther; that he was a descendant of Noah; to the theory that he was not Jewish at all, but still was a notably pious individual.

Some eighteen hundred years earlier, Sumer was an agricultural area supporting a number of city-states that were organized around temples; each city had its own deities and deep rivalry with the others. Scholars think Enheduanna's mother may have been Sumerian, while her father was Akkadian, a Semitic people from Akkad, northwest of the river valleys of Sumer. King Sargon united them militarily, and some of his daughter's other poetry, forty-two temple hymns in praise of each city's deities, helped to unify the region. In three long poems, Enheduanna exalted one goddess, Inanna, and told a personal story of her own exile and suffering.

I argue that her poetic story may have been carried out of Ur by Abraham and his group. Abraham and his wife Sarah, as literate people (Sarah was probably also a priestess), would have been educated with the writings of Enheduanna, since the poet's work was used to teach scribes literacy, in Ur and other Sumerian cities, for five hundred years following Enheduanna's death. This time line overlaps with the speculation that the Abrahamic peoples left Ur about 1800 BCE. They surely would have known Enheduanna's literature and her personal story of exile, suffering, and restitution, as well as the value of arguing with one's deity and of maintaining faith in the face of severest adversity.

Other Sumerian sacred stories have been recognized as contributing to biblical stories—including the creation sequences of Genesis, Noah and the Flood myth, and the episode of God choosing the offering of the shepherd over that of the farmer. This last story occurred in a Sumerian myth of Inanna choosing between two suitors (though without the murder of shepherd Abel by farmer Cain). The floating of the newborn Moses in a reed basket recycles a detail told of Enheduanna's father, Sargon. These Sumerian stories could have been carried out of Ur with Abraham's family, or any number of people moving west from Ur and migrating toward the shores of the Mediterranean.

Job's tale says he came from a place called "Uz." No one knows where Uz might have been. A Dead Sea Scroll note says Uz was "beyond the Euphrates," which also describes the location of Ur (after the river changed course). Uz occurs elsewhere in the Bible as the name of three or four men, but not as a place-name. My attention is caught by the fact that the words "Uz" and "Ur" are so similar, as are the Hebrew letters z and r, as though, miles and centuries from the original old city, a scribe or translator made a slight error.

This circumstantial reasoning is compelling, answering yes to the question of whether it would have been likely that, even as Sumerian language passed out of history and venerable old cities fell to dusty ruin, some Sumerian images, fragments, and entire stories, including Enheduanna's poetry, were carried westward. Changed, expanded, and absorbed into a sustained and lively Jewish oral as well as written tradition, the core teachings, because of their wisdom, would have been retained by Abraham and Sarah's descendants and eventually swept into the Tanakh collection as a part of sacred liturgy. Later, they were absorbed into Christian and Islamic holy writings, which also carried the ancient story into contemporary times. Lucky for every grieving, outraged person who ever used the story to get through an impossibly tough time.

Two Stories: Same Plot, Same Feelings

Setting aside the lengthy arguments that Job's friends have with him, and looking just at the core poetry telling the essential sequence of events, the two stories—one about Enheduanna's trials, the other about Job's—have a similar plot, but the order of telling is different.

Enheduanna's set of three poems begins with "Inanna and Ebih," describing the destruction of a mountain, Ebih, by the goddess. Inanna—"Lady of blazing dominion"—is determined to bring a perfectly stable, green, and luscious mountain down to its knees, to the horror of the Sky god, with whom she consults. Ignoring his advice, she vehemently (and with great detail in the telling) destroys Ebih, because, she says, it would not obey her, would not acknowledge her primacy.

Swift piercing, stinging
Fly with Inanna's fury
Suck loosened earth into sweet air

Dust chokes every blink and breath
Broken bits and fiery chips
Swirl in the dust-dark air

Following this cataclysmic event, the goddess builds herself a new temple and staffs it with personnel who are "head-overturned," meaning cross-gendered. (I will return to this later.)

In the second poem, Inanna is addressed as "Lady of Largest Heart" as the poet-priestess begins by describing some of her deity's powers. Only gradually does the poet allow us to know that she herself is in grief and anger over something. She is lamenting with the belief that tears would "cool" the goddess, whose anger is expressed through things going wrong.

Mistress
all day   every day weeping
you no longer roam the heavens
crying does not soothe your heart
stop I say
enough
moaning unending lamenting

Enheduanna is faithful to her goddess to the highest degree. Indeed, as the poet, she is the one who is elevating this goddess above all others, greater than the sky, greater than the wind, and, as she says to the goddess, "I have proclaimed you over the whole of the land."

Early in her account, the priestess begins expressing grief; she lets us know that an illness is upon her, and says to Inanna, "You allow my flesh to know your scourging." When she finally tells us details of her own personal story in the middle of the third poem, the details of her loss are that a man, a foe named Lugal-anne, has thrown her out of her temple. She has lost her station as high priestess and is dispossessed of everything. He reviles her person. He "wipes his spit-drenched hand" across her "honey-sweet mouth" and hands her a ritual knife of sacrifice or possibly laceration—i.e., a shamanic tool. The foe, probably a political rival, says, "This becomes you," as though to shame her.

Exiled, Enheduanna declares passionately that Inanna will save her; Inanna has the power to save her. She implores the goddess to intervene on her behalf, to "drive this man out / hunt him down." She challenges the goddess: "My sorrow and bitter trial / strike my eye as treachery." She stands up for herself: "I, I am Enheduanna . . . with single heart / I am devoted." Exiled and without social support, she becomes more desperate. She argues and pleads: "I say stop the bitter, hating heart." Inanna is the powerful one who can stop this pain. Enheduanna "wanders in thorny brush, in the mountains," far outside her city. She mourns her lost station in the temple, laments losing the rites she once performed with joy. "I no longer unravel [the moon's] gift of dreams / for anyone." She speaks of dying. Throughout, she continues to praise her goddess, describing vividly the various capacities and exploits of Inanna. She lists Inanna's paradoxical powers, the *mes*, ground rules for running society and nature that are contradictory. She declares her own righteousness, how she is the one who has exalted Inanna and proclaimed her glories throughout the land. Why then, she asks, is this happening to me? How long will this go on? Why won't you cool your heart for me?

Then she exalts Inanna to the highest imaginable power, queen over all the other gods, in a prayer that repeats:

Proclaim!
That you are more exalted than An [the Sky god]

Proclaim!
That you are wider than earth
Proclaim . . .
That your eyes flash like jewels
Proclaim!
That you balk and defy
Proclaim!
That you stand victorious
Proclaim!
. . . who alone are exalted

Enheduanna acknowledges that she is a "captive" of her goddess, and that she has a new understanding: "It is for my sake your anger fumes / your heart finds no relief." Following this, the goddess receives her prayer, restores her heart to Enheduanna, who is now returned to her temple and the position of high priestess. Inanna is then described: "She dresses lavishly / in woman's allure / . . . she glows with beauty's shine."

Enheduanna's emotional states go from grief, to outrage, to self-justification, and then to seeing Inanna as paradoxical, and great. The poet feels anger, desperation, fear, agony, lament for her losses, awe, humility, and renewal.

In Job's story, readers know from the first lines that Job is the most righteous of men, upstanding in his community, very wealthy, and "the greatest of all the men of the east." Job is a pious, honest man with whom God is not only pleased but extolling. The character of Satan intervenes in this verbal pleasure, goading God to take Job's wealth, family, and station, and then he will see that Job won't be so pious.

Consequently, Job loses his flocks, his house, and his wealth, and then he loses his children, when a monster wind crashes the roof onto them while they are attending a feast. In response to these terrible losses, Job falls to the ground and tears his robe in mourning. Yet even in his grief Job remains faithful, saying, "The Lord gives and takes away, blessed be the name of the Lord."

Satan tries again, asking God for permission to "touch his bone and skin," and then Job "will curse thee to thy face." God replies, basically, Okay, but don't kill him. Job now loses his health and breaks out in a skin rash, with boils all over his body. He sits down among ashes. He is seized with angry anguish, and curses the day that he was born: why did that day not shut up the doors to his mother's womb? "My flesh is clothed with worms and clods of dust; my skin is broken, and become loathsome." He is hopeless: "My days are swifter than a weaver's shuttle, and are spent without hope." He begins his argument with God; if he has sinned, Job asks, "Why not pardon my transgression?" He enumerates God's strength:

> *Which removeth the mountains, and they know not: which overturneth them in his anger.*
> *Which shaketh the earth out of her place, and the pillars thereof tremble.*
> *Which commandeth the sun, and it riseth not; and sealeth up the stars.*

He has run out of optimism: "He will suffer me to take my breath, but filleth me with bitterness." Acute cynicism sets in as Job loses all social respect, lives among garbage at the outskirts of town, and young men who once respected him hit him in the face and spit at him. He continues to describe his situation:

> *Know now that God hath overthrown me, and hath compassed me with his net.*

*Behold, I cry out of wrong, but I am not heard: I cry aloud, but there
is no judgment.*

*He hath fenced up my way that I cannot pass, and he hath set darkness
in my paths.*

He hath stripped me of my glory, and taken the crown from my head.

Now he challenges God, angrily defending himself:

*Is it good unto thee that thou shouldest oppress, that thou shouldest
despise the work of thine hands, and shine upon the counsel of the
wicked?*

Hast thou eyes of flesh? or seest thou as man seeth?

Are thy days as the days of man?

But Job also talks about the powers of the deity God, and
asks, what have I done wrong? Show me the reason for my suffering. Job admits to being afraid of God, that his flesh trembles.
Once again, he returns to his indomitable faith: "Though he slay
me, yet will I trust in him: but I will maintain mine own ways
before him." Job will not surrender his sense of righteousness.
Instead, he lists qualities of God that are paradoxical; God, he
realizes, "destroyeth the perfect and the wicked." Job compares
states of men's lives, always with the same end:

One dieth in his full strength, being wholly at ease and quiet . . .

And another dieth in the bitterness of his soul . . .

They shall lie down alike in the dust, and the worms shall cover them.

Job in despair, impoverished, ill and in pain, thinks about
his own death. He recalls the times when things were good,
when his children were around him, and the community respected him.

Oh that I were as in months past, as in the days when God preserved me;
When his candle shined upon my head, and when by his light I walked
through darkness.

Throughout his monologues, Job maintains that he has committed no sin, although his friends disagree about that in their arguments with him. Finally, God speaks out of the whirlwind, addressing Job directly in the well-known soliloquy:

Wilt thou also disannul my judgment? wilt thou condemn me, that thou
mayest be righteous?
Hast thou an arm like God? or canst thou thunder with a voice like him?

God continues, listing some of his powers and accomplishments, and comparing them with Job's inadequacy. Following this, Job agrees that he himself is insignificant, and God "turns his captivity," restores everything to him, even more than he had lost. Job lives a long, successful life.

Job's emotional states go from grief, to outrage, to self-justification, and then to seeing God as paradoxical, and great. Job feels anger, followed by desperation, fear, agony, lament for his losses, and then awe, humility, and restoration.

Overlapping Language Between the Two Texts

With such a vast amount of time between the two texts, and the vicissitudes of both oral and written traditions, translated across languages—and, as I imagine, transferred from clay tablets to rolled papyrus scrolls, passed along family lines and small religious sects—I was pleased as I compared Enheduanna with Job to find even a few overlapping identical nouns: lion, dragon, ashes, blood, eagle, bull, falcon or hawk, net, dreadful south wind, noon, noon with an eclipse or other darkness, and spit. These words are maybe not unusual in mythologies of this area of the world, but still some of them seem beyond coincidental. The phrases even more so.

For instance, both Inanna and God are described as "mountain-smashing." Enheduanna, as I said, devoted a long poem to Inanna's destruction of Mt. Ebih. The descriptions in the Bible of God as a mountain smasher are complex only in Job, and the phrasing is reminiscent of Inanna: "removes the mountain," "mountain is falling," and "overturns the mountain by its root."

How do the two texts describe their deity?

Enheduanna says: "She is changeable and hidden."

Job says: "When he hideth his face, who then can behold him?"

Enheduanna says: "What she crushes cannot be restored."

Job says: "Behold, he breaketh down, and it cannot be built again."

Enheduanna says: "She brings forth what is hidden into the light."

Job says: "He discovereth deep things out of darkness."

Enheduanna says: "I am yours / why do you slay me?"

Job says: "Thine hands have made me and fashioned me together round about; yet thou dost destroy me" and "though he slay me, yet will I trust in him."

Both deities have the broadest possible viewpoint, seeing both earth and heaven.

Inanna says:

my eyes scan the earth
I know the length of it

I travel heaven's pure road
I know the depth of it

Job says:

God understandeth the way thereof, and he knoweth the place thereof.
For he looketh to the ends of the earth, and seeth under the whole
*   heaven.*

Both texts end with a turn toward beauty.

In the last passages, Enheduanna says: "she dresses lavishly /
in woman's allure / . . . she glows with beauty's shine."

In the last passages, God says: "Deck thyself now with majesty
and excellency; and array thyself with glory and beauty."

Both deities are explicitly described as contradictory. How is
she paradoxical? Enheduanna says to Inanna:

You draw men into unending strife, or crown with fame
a favored person's life

to destroy   to build
to lift up   to put down
are yours Inanna

prosperous business   abundance of money
indebtedness   ruinous loss
are yours Inanna

to utter slander
words of deception . . .
to defile   to esteem . . .
are yours, Inanna

Inanna withdraws her heart and returns her heart.
Her heart heats up and can also be cooled.
She causes trembling illness and she also soothes and heals.
She takes away Enheduanna's high position, makes her poor,
then restores her to her high temple office.
How is God paradoxical?

"the Lord gave, and the Lord hath taken away;"
He makes a sore, and binds it up; he wounds and his hands make whole.
The deceived and deceiver are his
He looses the bonds of kings, and girds their loins with a girdle.
He increases the nations, and destroys them; he expands the nations and
*   narrows them again*

He takes away Job's prosperity, gives him poverty, then gives
him wealth again.

The two deities also have some similar powers with nature:
He withholds the waters and they dry up; he sends the waters
out and they overturn the earth.

She withholds water and there is drought, or she floods or overfloods the land.

Both deities protect the defenseless against the mighty, yet also bring about weakness.

Both deities create boundaries and also overrun them.

Both deities keep cosmic order, yet also bring about chaos.

One of the most often discussed moments in Job is when God speaks directly to him from "out of the whirlwind"—a highly unusual example of immanence, a characteristic of Inanna, but not of God. She takes different forms of nature, and for instance was addressed as "Mistress Falcon." God would not be addressed as "Mister Falcon." As creator he is separate from nature, and he does not occupy its forms to speak—except when he speaks from a bush in Exodus, and in his final sequence out of the whirlwind in Job; the grand speech God then makes is a turning point in the story.

So, my burning question: While there is a whirlwind accompanying Inanna in another of her myths, is there a whirlwind reference in Enheduanna's poetry? Yes. She directly refers to Inanna as "a whirlwind warrior" in Betty's translation; in the ETCSL translation Inanna is "clothed in a whirlwind." So Inanna could also be said to speak "out of the whirlwind."

I've listed quite a few parallels above, and there are more.

Enheduanna mentioned the older gods (the Annunaki), Stone Age gods who were still present in the new Bronze Age. She wrote of Mt. Ebih:

the gods . . .
bend with fear of Ebih
. . . [the gods]
tremble, stricken
their flesh prickles all over

We wouldn't expect "gods" to appear in the Book of Job, as this contradicts monotheism. Nevertheless there is a translation of "the gods" fearing Leviathan. Usually the translations say "the mighty," but one says this:

even the gods are afraid of it—
Even the gods [are] overwhelmed at the sight of it . . .
When it raises itself up the gods are afraid; at the crashing they are beside themselves.

The voices used in both works make dramatic use of the literary devices of the first-, second-, and third-person narrative. Enheduanna tells her own story in the first person: "But that man cast me among the dead," and "with single heart I am devoted." She speaks of Inanna in the third person: "Wild bull Queen / mistress of brawn / boldly strong. / no one dares turn away." The poet also addresses the goddess directly, employing the second person: "You all knowing / You wise vision / Lady of all lands . . . / You of the bountiful heart."

Job tells some of his own story in the first person: "I put on righteousness, and it clothed me." Job speaks of God in the third person, as in "For what is the hope of the hypocrite, though he hath gained, when God taketh away his soul?" Job also addresses him directly: "I know that thou canst do everything, and that no thought can be withholden from thee."

In both works, the two deities speak for themselves in certain parts. Inanna has a dialogue with the Sky god An: "You are he who / gives my word weight / over all others." She describes herself: "I come forth a queen / like cool moonlight / down the breast of the sky." She directly scolds the mountain: "You thick-hided elephant!"

God speaks out of the whirlwind, telling his powers, beginning with the challenge: "Hast thou an arm like God? or canst thou thunder with a voice like him?," speaking of himself in the third person, which is a little precious, given the grandiosity of the declarations. Then he says directly to Job's friends, "My wrath is kindled against thee."

In both cases, the combination of these literary techniques helps produce narratives of high drama and emotion.

Coming back to the two protagonists, the plot sequences of their suffering are identical, and the lessons they learn are as well.

Toward the end of Enheduanna's story, after she has been awed by the greatness of Inanna's powers, she acknowledges a new humility:

I
who am I
in the place which holds up
life's key elements

Toward the end of Job's story, after he has been awed by the greatness of God's powers, he also acknowledges a new humility. He has spoken rashly, as there were "wondrous things I did not know," and he says humbly, "I see that I am insignificant."

Near the end of her story, Enheduanna says, "I am your *captive*" to Inanna; after that, she is restored to her temple and her office of high priestess.

Near the end of Job's story, God "turns his captivity" in restoring Job to his wealth, prestige, community, and family.

So, closely examining the poetry reveals a great deal of similarity, even exact parallels, within both stories, including in descriptions of the two deities. Both of them are the ultimate power in the cosmos, and both of the suffering humans make their way through their feeling states to a thorough understanding of this.

Both of the deities create "darkness at noon." This could mean a solar eclipse, or it could refer to a sky filled with ash and smoke. Which brings me to the crucial point that both Inanna and God are "mountain smashers."

Mountain Smashers: Ebih and Leviathan

Ebih

Enheduanna's first long poem describes her goddess demolishing a mountain. Inanna's beauty is her primary characteristic; she both magnetizes and radiates desire. It's very shocking to read about this young, vibrant, seductively beautiful goddess of love and sexuality (as so much of her other poetry portrays her) suddenly picking up weapons and destroying an entire, glorious mountain. Mt. Ebih is green and luscious, full of fruit trees and wild animals. Why on earth would she do that? "I attack the mountain," she declares, and she "wrestles the mountain to its knees / stands the victor at its base."

Inanna is a natural force with the power to destroy a mountain through fire. That Inanna wields that fire is clear from the opening line, in which the poet Enheduanna describes Inanna as "blazing":

Lady of blazing dominion
clad in dread
riding on fire red power

Inanna is even dressed as "flame" as she rides out to battle the mountain:

on her smooth brow she paints
fire beams and fearsome glint

fastens carnelian
blood-red and glowing
around her throat

She says, "I spread terror all down the mountain," and she showers "the land with flames of fire" and "spins ash around the city gates"; her voice "howls and shrieks."

In her attack on the mountain, Inanna makes the earth shake, sets the mountain aflame (using the fire god Gibil), and causes stony landslides with "evil silt." Far more devastation than a simple forest fire is at work in Enheduanna's poem. The lush mountain is suddenly subject to hurricane-force winds, to drought and fire, and to landslides sending boulders tumbling "down the flanks," as though the mountain were a great beast with haunches. The sky turns dark at noon, stones are sucked into the sky, flames and smoke are everywhere, trees collapsing, rocks tumbling down, rivers drying up, grasses burning, until the mountain ultimately, as Inanna claims, has been grabbed by its horns, "brought to its knees," and "melted like a vat of sheep's fat." (Sheep's fat refers to tallow, used as fuel in lamps.)

That group of images, many of them ranging throughout Enheduanna's poetry, unmistakably describes a volcanic episode. Nothing else beside red-hot lava flow "melts" a mountain of rocky earth. Nothing else changes a high mountain into a "clay bowl," which describes a caldera. Nothing else in nature brings a mountain "to its knees" and "to the ground," by reducing its size and shape.

For the poets of the Sumerian people, mountain smashing was not a geological event. For them it was a battle between living forces, as every mountain, every plant, even every stone, was a sentient, alive being.

"Mountain!" the goddess cries, "I have killed you! / I have struck your heart with sorrow!"

The killing of Mt. Ebih happens when Inanna sets the volcanic fire. She *is* the power of destruction, *is* the force that melts the mountain. She is immanent as the greatest imaginable force of the times—"Lady Dragon," as Enheduanna calls her.

In contemporary science, we see the eruption, the ebb and flow of hot magma, as a matter of natural forces: pressure, gases, the water table dropping, tectonic shifts, and so on. With our geological knowledge, we speak of a lava-spewing mountain as a volcano; we don't separate the fire from the mountain. The Sumerians saw them each as a living spirit; they did not see the force of the internal fire and the stony, forested surface of the mountain as the same being. Rather, they saw the mountain *attacked* by the fiery force. The poetry suggests they thought the fiery force came down from above, not that it erupted out of the center. Inanna "pressed the dagger's teeth into its interior." In Enheduanna's poem, the fiery force is wielded by Inanna, and she is credited with "killing" the mountain. The poet is trying to explain why this would have happened.

Were there volcanoes anywhere near ancient Sumer? Yes. Ebih is named even today as a mountain or range in the Diyala River region of the Zagros Mountains. It possibly underwent a volcanic upheaval several thousand years ago. The Zagros ranges, just east of the Tigris River, formed a border of Sumer. They are full of volcanic cones from distant times. These mountains are situated on a tectonic fault that remains active, and volcanoes have erupted into modern times. Volcanoes are usually accompanied by large and small earthquakes, causing the land to quiver, a repeated imagery related to Inanna's capacity to spread terror: "You made the place tremble," and "all heaven trembles at your word." Volcanic plumes can also feature dramatic lightning storms, another "weapon" in Inanna's arsenal.

Inanna destroyed Ebih with volcanic force. Is there such a force in Job? Given how deeply imprinted this story is in Enheduanna's account, we could expect that this part of her story also carried over to the later tale.

For God, of course, since he is outside of nature, a volcanic force would not "be" God, but rather would take the imaginary form of some being under God's control. Is such a creature in the story of Job? Yes.

Leviathan

A ferocious creature named Leviathan receives about thirty-four lines of attention at a crucial point in the Book of Job. Leviathan is usually interpreted today as a thick-skinned, large, and very real animal—a crocodile, hippopotamus, or rhinoceros. However, this interpretation underestimates our hunting ancestors. Forty thousand years ago in icy Europe, Cro-Magnon and Neanderthal hunters crept bravely up on mastodons, woolly mammoths, and fifteen-hundred-pound aurochs with stone-tipped weapons and their own grit. In Africa hunters for tens of millennia courageously faced all the large, fierce animals of that continent with spears tipped with sharp stone, then sharp iron.

And there are even more current examples. In Uganda in 2015, a fifty-five-year-old man slayed a twenty-five-foot long crocodile that had killed his wife and other women in his village; he used a barbed spear with a rope attached and fought the beast for an hour and a half. Oh Leviathan, if you were a crocodile, how easily you'd go down in real life. So I don't agree with the animal imagery for this monster. Leviathan, in my interpretation, is a volcano: a very real force of nature, still terrifying, still today out of any kind of human control.

Leviathan, as a "sea serpent," is fire in the water. Volcanic and tectonic activity is imagined as a "dragon" and earth energy as a "snake" in widespread locations, from India and other parts of Asia to the western United States (according to indigenous peoples there). God says of Leviathan that smoke comes from his nostrils, as if out of a boiling pot; his breath kindles coals, and flames come from his mouth. His heart is stone, hard as the base of a millstone; no weapons can hold in him, and iron is to him like straw, brass like rotten wood. He spreads sharp pointed things among the muck. All this is extremely suggestive of volcanic lava, which leaves sharp-edged cinders on top of the gray mass as it cools. Ancient warriors who shot arrows and flung spears into lava tongues would find their weapons dissolved. Leviathan, as molten lava, pours his heat into the sea, making it boil, and making the water look like a "pot of ointment," a red cosmetic. On land as well as at the seashore, he makes "a hoary path that shines" as he goes along (hoary means "silvery white," a characteristic of recently cooled lava, including in the sea). "Upon earth there is not his like," the Job poet says. He's no mere rhinoceros. When Hawaiian volcano Kilauea spills into the sea, as the goddess Pele, she leaves just such a path of shining white—that is, brand-new land.

In the Job story, perhaps completed as a text somewhere near the Mediterranean Sea, thirteen hundred miles west of the Euphrates, Leviathan goes into water, making it boil "like a cauldron." By this time of the setting of the Job story, in the era of brass, between 1400 BCE and around 600 BCE, people would know about the historic collapse of the mountain on the island of Santorini in the eastern Mediterranean, and other volcanic activities near the sea. Santorini blew up about 1600 BCE; the island is only about six hundred miles from Lebanon and Israel. Travelers of the era would have heard details about this, the most destructive volcanic eruption in human history.

Leviathan fits the description of an active volcanic mountain, whose "mouth" (vent) breathes sparks of fire like burning lamps, and whose nose emits smoke. If I am correct in my poet's interpretation of the imagery, then Leviathan and Mt. Ebih were both volcanoes, and both were considered by the ancient poets to have consciousness—especially, to possess willfulness.

Each represents the same qualities theologically. The Sumerian poet made clear the lesson of why the fierce goddess would slay a mountain—because of its beauty, because of its abundance, and because of its arrogance in not recognizing her:

Because you puff yourself up
because you stand so high
dress up so beautiful

And because Ebih does not "press lips to the dust" in acknowledgment of Inanna's power, she says, "Mountain, I have killed you!" The mountain has pride, stubbornness, and rebellion.

In Job, it is the voice of God who describes Leviathan as a monster, making the point that only God's power could control such a ferocious beast, a beast that is dragonlike, scaly, toothy, and breathing fire. Leviathan is interpreted, by theologians and storefront preachers alike, as "the king over all the children of pride," as one translation states.

Ebih is accused of the same quality.

The Job story carries some of the moral as well as geological lessons of Enheduanna's goddess. Leviathan and Ebih are parallel beings with similar characteristics and meanings in the two stories. Both of them represent hubris—pride, stubbornness, rebellion, refusal to accept the authority of the deity.

So God and Inanna are both credited with the fiery monster (God through creation, Inanna through immanence); and both are credited with taming it by "smashing it." Taming Leviathan is the culminating and most impressive power God cites for himself, following which Job becomes humble. Crediting Inanna with such a tumultuous calamity as a volcano is the last step in her transition from a minor to a major deity, and something Enheduanna continued to bring up numerous times in citing the goddess's many powers and accomplishments. In her concluding praise of Inanna, the poet lists three qualities: the smashing of the mountain; the acquisition of the *mes*, or "unchanging powers"; and the goddess being "wrapped in beauty."

Differences: Sin, Satan, and Sex

Sin

The most obvious difference between Enheduanna and Job is that while the Sumerian poet's story of loss appears to be autobiographical, certain aspects of the biblical book appear to be those of a fable. These include details of Job's wealth and family, and the dialogues he has with his three "comforters" plus a fourth young man. The family details use magical numbers 7, 3, and 10. His great wealth includes 7000 sheep and 3000 camels. He has 10 children, of whom 7 are sons and 3 are daughters. The sons have a 7-day celebration in which a wind blows the roof down, killing them all. Job mourns for 7 days and 7 nights. When God chastises Job's friends at the end of the story, he requires them to sacrifice 7 bulls and 7 rams. When Job regains a family, his children are again 10 in number, 7 sons and 3 daughters.

Job's four comforters act as his critics, arguing in opposition to him in lengthy dialogues within which Job is able to present himself as a righteous man, a compassionate, generous man, a man faithful to his wife as well as his God.

The three friends take turns urging him to say what his sins have been. Bildad says to Job that if he were "pure and upright," surely God would make him prosperous: "God will not cast away a perfect man, neither will he help the evildoers."

Job contests this, concluding that "He destroyeth the perfect and the wicked." (The Jerusalem Bible uses "innocent" rather than "perfect.")

The friends who engage him in argument seem to be a literary device for the purpose of extending the discussion of not only *why* good men suffer, but even *if* good men suffer—that is to say, if you lose everything, it must surely be because of something you have done wrong, so you are no longer "good." This philosophical position leads to the poor and disabled becoming pariahs, their losses accounted for as alleged sin. Conversely, this also applies to those who for various reasons—mentally ill, epileptic, or homosexual—have been labeled pariahs, and therefore are considered sinful. Does God punish people for conditions of their lives? Some fundamentalists publicly declaim that hurricanes, floods, and other disasters and tragedies indicate a society "lax" in its morals, meaning especially sexual behaviors. The arguments in Job circle around such ideas.

Job is very concerned with holding the line with his contentious friends, denying that he is guilty of anything. He defends those people who are unfortunate and suffering. He declares his despair and suffering at length, yet he maintains his own ways. The three old friends, joined late in the story by a younger man, become angry with him for maintaining his righteousness. Then God speaks out of the whirlwind (as part of nature) and describes his own powers at length, ending with his control over the fire monster Leviathan. Job is humbled. But he does not admit to any sin. Instead, he says there were wondrous things he did not know and finds himself "insignificant" in the face of God's greatness.

In the King James version and a few others, however, the term used is "vile," which sounds as though Job despises himself. I don't understand why this isn't changed, because "vile" in its archaic (and contemporary Hebrew) meaning is simply "of little worth," not the extremely bad things it means now.

Sin is not a factor in Enheduanna's account, although Betty Meador did translate one line as "What is my iniquity?" Job has this line as well, but the sense is not a confession. Instead, it is challenging the deity to say what the wrongdoing might have been, in the sense of, why are you doing all this tough stuff to me? "Iniquity" can mean "off the path."

Inanna destroys what angers her and blesses with abundance what pleases her; the mountain-smashing story makes clear that Inanna's rage was set off by the lack of respect shown by the mountain. But the individual act of breaking religious law, such as Cain's murder of his brother, or Job's possibly secretly cursing God as his friends accuse—this kind of "sinfulness" is missing in Enheduanna's text.

The text of Job is longer because of the addition of lengthy arguments with his four friends, whom he calls "miserable comforters," blaming him for his situation and wanting him to acknowledge his sin. He remains firm in his sense of innocence, and eventually the friends give up, claiming that Job has added rebellion to his sin because he will not give in to their judgments.

God sides with Job's interpretation that he is innocent, and levies a fine against the friends, who he says have been in folly and have not spoken correctly. The friends didn't understand, though Job did:

> *And it was so, that after the Lord had spoken these words unto Job, the Lord said to E-li-phaz the Te-man-ite, My wrath is kindled against thee, and against thy two friends: for ye have not spoken of me the thing that is right, as my servant Job hath . . .*
> *And the Lord turned the captivity of Job . . . the Lord gave Job twice as much as he had before.*

Where does morality fit with this? The lesson in Enheduanna and, later, in the Book of Job teaches that righteousness does not save a person from trouble. However, staying true to oneself and one's sense of living in goodness (which includes caring for others and fulfilling one's obligations) matters over all else. For both protagonists their suffering is resolved, even through despair, by staying in dialogue with, and in awe of, creation. By being honest we avoid the pitfalls of dishonesty and hypocrisy, which undermine the self and its connections. And, by not judging, not using the concept of "sin" against self or others, we remain compassionate toward fellow beings, knowing that anyone can be wiped out socially and economically, and anyone can be subject to illness. So the world-view mitigates cruelty and self-cruelty.

In Enheduanna, deity is the intersection (or interaction) between humanity and nature. Not an order above and beyond nature, but the intelligence, beauty, and energetic forces within nature. And nature cannot be bribed:

> who dares oppose
> your deeds
> Queen of Heaven and Earth
>
> no bribes sway
> divine verdicts you say
> Inanna
> judge of the palace throng . . .
>
> you alone are glorious
> all gods
> all heaven and earth
> call you Great Mother Cow

The Sumerians' view of Inanna also includes her compassion and, in her immanence, travel through every province of existence. Inanna might show up anywhere, in any form. From hymns to Inanna that were also written by Enheduanna, we learn that the goddess sometimes wears "a single garment like the nameless poor," "and drinks from puddles with the dogs." She "shares a stall with the horses" in the stable. Inanna may wear a necklace of pearls "of the prostitute" around her neck and slips into the tavern "like a ghost" where she "might snatch a man." These lines, taken from a number of hymns to her, make it clear just what a shape-shifter Inanna was to Sumerians, likely to be present in any situation, among any group of beings, human and creature alike. Another poem mentions a mother placing a sick child in Inanna's arms. Mercy, compassion, and pity are values of Inanna's, and therefore of the poet Enheduanna as well.

Compassion toward the poor is also attributed to Job. He lists his merits as caring for widows and the poor:

> *Because I delivered the poor that cried, and the fatherless, and him that had none to help him.*
> *The blessing of him that was ready to perish came upon me: and I caused the widow's heart to sing for joy.*
> *I put on righteousness, and it clothed me: my judgment was as a robe and a diadem.*
> *I was eyes to the blind, and feet was I to the lame.*
> *I was a father to the poor: and the cause which I knew not I searched out.*

Job's view of the poor around him in his downfall includes not necessarily blaming them for their station in life. He sees God as contradictory rather than meting out punishment and reward for loyalty. Job and Enheduanna share a remarkable viewpoint, a morality that hinges on love and awe rather than fear and a sense of superiority or guilt.

Satan vs. Foe

The characterizations of the villains in these two stories are quite different. Satan as a supernatural force for evil has developed along these lines especially in Christian doctrine, hundreds of years after the Job story was swept into the Tanakh. Later, Satan became identified with the snake in the Garden of Eden story; later still, he was identified with Lucifer, and the goat god of European paganism. But in Job, in 400 BCE, he is described only as a tempter; in Job he acts as a tormentor, bent on revealing an inner weakness in his victim, and Job's triumph is in not letting this happen.

For Enheduanna's drama, the adversary is a military man, a usurper who invades her temple, insults her, and displaces her. For some researchers, his wiping a spit-stained hand across her "honey sweet mouth" raises the specter of possible rape. But this interpretation seems contradicted by him then handing her the "knife of mutilation" (or sacrifice) with the words "This becomes you," as though he is humiliating her as a priestess rather than as a woman. Perhaps he belonged to a faction rebelling against the rule of Enheduanna's father, Sargon, as Betty Meador suggests. Whoever he was, he is named in the poem—Lugal-anne—and he is an ordinary human being, a foe.

Interestingly, that is what Satan means as well; the literal translation from the Hebrew of the term "satan" is "foe," "adversary," "one who obstructs."

So Satan is an ordinary adversarial foe, not a supernatural force (let alone something with snake and goat features). But in Job, Satan is a supernatural being who whispers into God's ear, has God's confidence, and scalds Job with illness. This opened the way for the development, over the centuries (especially in the New Testament and in medieval times), of the idea of Satan as an archetype of projection. This projection, cloaked in whatever is deemed "evil," has been used to dehumanize entire groups, such as Jews, Roma, Muslims, homosexuals, and the indigenous peoples of Europe, Africa, and the Americas.

Sex

Sex is barely mentioned in Job, and then it is because a question is raised about his fidelity to his marriage. He replies somewhat vehemently:

I made a covenant with mine eyes . . .
why then should I think upon a maid? . . .
If mine heart have been deceived by a woman, or I have laid wait at my
*   neighbour's door;*
Then let my wife grind unto another, and let others bow down upon her.

The wife does not appear to be a real person in that passage, but symbolic of—even a pawn in—the idea of sexual fidelity. Job's wife, who stays with him throughout the ordeal of their losses, is cast as a tempter, suggesting her husband "curse God and die" when his suffering is most acute. In one clue that she is part of the fable, she and Job start with ten children, lose them, and then have ten more when Job is restored to God's favor. This means the poor woman would have borne twenty children—I hope not.

There are several times when femaleness is critiqued and even disparaged in Job. To his wife, Job says, "You speak as one of the foolish women speak." He also says, "Man that is born of a woman is of few days, and full of trouble."

Bildad, one of Job's friends, says, "How can man be clean that is born of a woman?" Another of the friends, Eliphaz, says: "What is man, that he should be clean? and he which is born of a woman, that he should be righteous?" Meaning that just to be born "of woman" is automatically to be unclean and sinful. There is nothing like this in Enheduanna's poetry, and Sumerian poetry in general does not convey a sense of original sin, let alone that "woman" is to blame for people's suffering on earth. Quite the contrary: Sumerian poets revered the mother goddesses. In the millennia following the disappearance of Sumerian culture, as patriarchal values and ritual swung into primacy, the positive, benevolent, and life-giving powers of menstruation and other female energetic expressions fell away. The negative, though greatly reduced (no more causing of rain or determining fates), remained in place. The misogyny of claiming men as "unclean" because "born of woman" is clearly about a new and prejudicial notion of women's blood pollution.

Menstruating women had long been understood as capable of diminishing and distracting male powers, and the accompanying energies of bleeding could interfere with foodstuffs and processes of all kinds. Following childbirth as well as during menses, women were expected to stay in seclusion and ritually "cleanse" themselves of disturbance effects. The Adam and Eve story fixed in a limited place woman's sexuality, autonomy, and formerly generative menstrual rituals. Her relation to sentient beings in nature—exemplified by Snake—became a target of God's wrath, resulting in the expelling of the primal parents from the original garden. The concept that the consequence of Eve's disobedience means that everyone is born into a state of "sin" is central to the arguments put forward by Job's friends. And Job, holding to the older meaning of the older text, remains adamant that he has done nothing to deserve his pain.

In Enheduanna's poetry, the deity curses and blesses, is strident when moving around and calm when seated, can be open- or closed-hearted, receiving or rejecting. But nowhere is there a sign of "original sin" or that women are "unclean." In Inanna's mythology overall, the sense of right behavior includes being responsible to the land and interactive with its life-forms, who might be (at any given moment) the goddess herself. Through her faith and her rituals, the priestess Enheduanna sees herself as "partner" to the goddess, at the same time learning as she goes through vicissitudes of life that she is both encompassed by and "captive" of the forces of nature.

Enheduanna, though enraged with the foe who insulted and displaced her, does not displace her anger onto maleness.

Rather, she declares her loyalty to the other gods, the Sky god An and the Moon god Nanna. Although sex as such is not mentioned in Enheduanna's three long poems, Inanna is the most highly erotic of deities. The Inanna of explicit love rites, of sensuous beauty, of her lavishly described bed of love; the young Inanna demanding her own satisfaction in detail, sneaking out at night and lying to her mother in order to spend time with her lover, the bull god—all are backdrop to the Inanna of volcanic power. However, in telling her own story, Enheduanna is concerned with other matters: the seriousness of Inanna's powers, and of her own fragilities in the face of personal loss. Nevertheless, Inanna's tenderness shines through, as do her power of enabling happy marriage, her sweetness toward babies, and her providing of abundance: "To build a house / construct the women's rooms / furnish them / to kiss a baby's lips / are yours, Inanna."

Inanna's approach to gender, including a third and fourth category of gender, is very present. In fact, it's emphasized in this work—seventy lines are devoted to descriptions of Inanna's capacities to change human gender and create new gender categories, in a ritual Betty Meador translated as "head-overturning."

Head-Overturning and the Androgyny of Inanna

The most surprising difference between Enheduanna's poetry and the story of Job is the head-overturning ritual—changing gender: woman into man, and man into woman—which is referred to three times in Enheduanna's poetry. There is not a whisper of this ritual in Job.

Immediately after melting Mt. Ebih, Inanna builds herself a new temple, and brings in personnel:

Summon a *kurgarra* for holy office
Bestow the sacred implements
Holy mace and dagger

Summon a *gala*, singer of lamentation
Dispense the tools of office
Kettle drum and hand drum

Summon holy attendants
For ritual head-overturning
Priest to become woman
Priestess to become man

A long passage about head-overturning describes first a "manly-hearted woman" changed ritually into a man warrior, when Inanna "consecrates the maiden's heart as male." Inanna's ritual of head-overturning changes the social construction of gender. The head-overturned are given tools of the opposite sex, a mace to the manly-hearted woman and a woman's brooch to the man. They are named *pilipili* and given shamanic office as temple personnel. In an earlier myth, *pilipili*, who use ecstatic trance, lamentations, singing, and drumming to rouse energies, accompany Inanna in her quest for justice.

Other Sumerian names for androgynous, cross-dressed, or hermaphroditic people were *galaturra* and *kurgarra*; they also performed elegies and lamentations in Inanna's temple. They spoke or sang in Emesal, the women's dialect, and from all indications had homosexual intercourse. The scholar Will Roscoe found explicit same-sex erotic references to both *galaturra* and *kurgarra* (female *salkurgarra*) in other contexts. Since erotic energy is one of Inanna's powers, there is every reason to suppose that the manly-hearted women also had lesbian relations if so inclined.

In Inanna's descent myth, as I said earlier, a *kurgarra* and a *gala-turra* effected Inanna's rescue and return from the underworld, bringing her the water of life and the plant of life to resurrect her from her dead state.

As temple personnel, they held sacred office and designated occupations in society. They participated in crisis and transition rites, performed at New Year's festival and eclipse ceremonies, and functioned as lamentation singers. The *galaturra* both enacted and calmed the goddess's anger; they made offerings, served at funerary functions. The *kurgarru* dissolved evil, wore on occasions the mask of the goddess, provided charms against witchcraft, read omens, recited poetry, and played the flute and several kinds of drum. Under Inanna's cloak of protection, their sexual orientation enhanced her project of infusing the land with sacred erotic energy. The *pilipili, kurgarru,* and *gala* helped Inanna's precinct by expressing appropriate and public emotion. They drummed and danced to bring on ecstatic trance states of openness to cosmic energies. They were like artists in that sense, and with guaranteed succor. (I'll take it!)

Nothing like sin or disapproval seems attached to these sacred offices, although Betty Meador translated a part of the head-overturning ritual with lines detailing that the "manly-hearted" woman was experiencing social disapproval or some other "great punishment" that was removed by the gender-changing ritual, which also "shifted a god's curse." Which god is not specified, nor what the "curse" might have entailed.

Inanna
dressing a maiden
within the women's rooms
embraces with full heart
the young girl's handsome bearing

the maid a woman evilly spurned
taunted to her face
sways beneath the wrath
thrown at her everywhere . . .

this dreadful state
the Lady would undo
take the scourge
from her burdened flesh

over the maiden's head
she makes a sign of prayer
hands then folded at her nose
she declares her manly/woman

The sequence of events in Enheduanna's work begins with the mountain smashing, and a crediting of Inanna, who had been a minor goddess, with a major geological event. Perhaps volcanic activity has never been so explicitly described—explained, really—as something within human understanding: the goddess of high energies did it. This event is followed by a ten-line description of head-overturning.

According to Enheduanna's poem, a change in the geography has just occurred, implying that having a stable, verdant mountain suddenly spew fire and ash and "melt" into a new formation led to Inanna's priesthood staffing her new temple with cross-gendered, probably homosexual personnel. Maybe this has a logic to it. A transformation in the human understanding of mysterious, frightening eruptions in the land around them had happened and the relationship of Sumerians to nature required new explanation. And just as in current times, when natural or human crises are newly understood and newly dangerous, homosexual and cross-gendered people become visible, even prominent; throughout the ages, it's as though society senses that new sensibilities and new rituals are needed to deal with new knowledge and dangerous circumstances.

The close description of how Inanna went about head-overturning first the manly-hearted woman and then the man (who had scorned the goddess) ends with her naming them "reed-marsh woman, reed-marsh man." She gives them names of a specific geographic location. Why would she do that?

The twin rivers, Tigris and Euphrates, flow from the high northern mountains of Mesopotamia down to the Persian Gulf, culminating in a broad stretch of marshlands, which until recent political devastation were home to numerous fisher people. The rich sediment and mixture of salt and fresh waters produced seafood and bird life galore, and tall reeds with which the marshland population made houses and beautiful crescent-shaped boats. Why would a poet say that the goddess named her cross-gendered people after this area?

Perhaps the answer is hiding in the origin story of the first generation of Sumerian gods, a gendered story of creation through separation of the elements from each other, as male and female pairs. The Sky (male An) and the Earth (female Ki) separated; next the Ocean (female Nammu) and the fresh river waters (male Enki) separated. That is to say, the myth named these elements and thereafter people could "see" them in a storied way and honor them distinctly. The marshlands are a mix of earth, ocean water, and river water, and therefore a mix of creation genders.

By saying that Inanna had named the *pilipili* for the marshlands, the high priestess-poet was not only giving them sacred office in the temple as shamanic ritualists, but also weaving them into the central origin story itself. It is as though biblical texts said that God brought cross-gendered characters into the Adam and Eve story, named them Tree of Knowledge and Sacred Spring, and said, "This part of the Garden of Eden is yours."

Inanna's homosexual and transgendered shamanic temple personnel followed her in her quest for justice—they accompanied her along with a whirlwind. She has everything to do with weather, and so of course they would be connected to this capacity as well. I bring this up because of the bizarre beliefs of some Christian evangelicals that homosexuality brings on hurricanes and floods. For them this is about a god being angry with alleged disobedience, but I'm wondering if the connection didn't simply travel down the lineage, starting with gay and lesbian and trans (cross-gendered) shamanic priests in service to the powerhouse weather goddess. In my experience with contemporary goddess rituals, priest-shamans actually do have connections with weather—especially wind and rainfall. But earthquakes, hurricanes, and volcanoes? Nah. For that we need Inanna's power.

Inanna too is cross-gendered, in the sense that she holds both the cloak of women and the mace of men. The androgyny of Inanna is a consequence of astronomical Sumerian observers understanding that they were tracking one single entity, that the third brightest light in the western sky at night was the same as the third brightest light in the eastern sky at dawn. In the broad, mountainous northern and southeastern borders of the Mesopotamian region, some people had mythologized the morning star as a male warrior; for others, importance was given the evening star as female, associated with love and beauty. The combination of warrior and lover became the goddess Inanna—and the new concept of a planet with its own unique course, which included disappearing from the western sky and reappearing in the east. Perhaps the connection was affirmed by seeing one bright golden light with eight distinctive rays coming from the center. The eight-pointed star became Inanna's earliest and most pervasive signature.

In ancient India, in a sister culture to ancient Mesopotamia, the kind of fire that Inanna represents is called Shakti, who is also a goddess in her own right. The north Indian goddess Durga has similar characteristics. As the primeval mother of the cosmos, Durga created matter, and when the countryside was besieged by a demon who wanted to usurp the people, she sat on a lion and let out a roar that set the oceans roiling and volcanoes exploding. In contemporary India, nuclear tests in the 1990s were named Shakti, and atomic energy sites have Shakti as part of their name, clearly associating her with the infinite energy in basic atoms.

In some of Inanna's other poetry, sexual fire was her province, expressed in her prolific love poetry, and also her "Cult Prostitute." Inanna was the essence of conviviality, with a sacred bed in the tavern and a ritual of drinking beer with her human priests. Sexuality—eros—is the first principle of aesthetic beauty, of intuitive knowing, of glowing attraction and health, and of vivacity and fecundity of every kind, including intellectual and artistic. With her elevation by Enheduanna to the power level of volcanic fire, Inanna became also a creator of, and a destroyer of, land itself.

Inanna is androgynous in the sense that in combining the morning-star warrior with the evening-star lover, her powers are a mix of female and male rituals, and she is surrounded by reed-marsh women and reed-marsh men. She became extremely powerful, but not a creator of "everything"—which would separate her from nature. She was part of a pantheon in which all the gods together played their parts. In Inanna, as Enheduanna portrayed her, Sumerians created an androgynous deity, just one step and about ten centuries away from setting the firmament in place, having the kind of cosmos-creating power that would be attributed to a monotheistic, masculine god.

Righteous Truth-Telling Outrage

To summarize the argument that the story of Inanna provided the basis for the Book of Job, let me consider the evidence. When Abraham and Sarah came out of the city of Ur around 1800 BCE, they carried with them the poetry of the high priestess Enheduanna, whose work had been used to teach literacy to scribes in Sumer for more than five hundred years. No one knows who wrote the Book of Job, although scholars agree that much of it is fable, surrounding core poetry that tells the essential story. My comparison of words and phrases reveals overlapping beyond what could be coincidental. The plots of events that happen to both protagonists are virtually identical, including the emotional states they experience. Both the episode of Inanna "melting" Mt. Ebih and the description of Leviathan spewing fire surely describe what we call volcanic activity. Both works are teaching a theology of paradox. Both resolutions happen after the protagonists relinquish their ego-identification with their own suffering, and acknowledge their own limitations in the face of the greatness of creation.

In writing her own story, Enheduanna produced a morality tale for the ages, and she did it out of an urgent need for justice, and adoration of her deity. Her duties were to the temple of the moon couple (Nanna and Ningal), where among other things she performed dream divination. She also frequently expressed her devotion to the Sky god An. But clearly she fell completely in love with the golden planet her people had long called Inanna, "Lady Brilliance." In Betty Meador's translation, the priestess called to the goddess, "O my wild, ecstatic cow!" and said she herself was Inanna's spouse. That intense love led her to exalt to the utmost the qualities of the inner, erotic, creative fire, both humanly passionate and volcanically explosive, both animating of life and crushing of it, both smashing of parts of the land and creating it, both murderous and renewing. That love led Enheduanna to have faith that even in her personal suffering and exile, the power of her adoration and awe for her deity, engaged in dialogue through the art of poetry, would enable her to keep her own sense of self, to eventually be restored as high priestess, and to continue serving her people.

Enheduanna's autobiography, written on clay more than 4100 years ago and later converted into a masculine form retaining much of her story, some of her poetry, and most of her theology, has permeated the world. Well over 50 percent of all people on earth belong to religions that include the story of Job. I'm guessing that hundreds of millions of people have been able to identify with this poignant story in order to tame their volatile emotions during crises, and to survive disaster and loss without harming anyone. In addition, Enheduanna produced a theology of contradiction, mirroring the paradoxical characteristics of nature and therefore deifying truth and life circumstance without demonizing. She described human gender changes remarkably similar to those we are experiencing today and gave cross-gendered people third-gender names and a place in the sacred precinct of elements, as well as functions in Inanna's temple. She also named and described an energetic force, ascribed to Inanna, that could melt mountains, adding to the understanding of what would eventually become geological science, as well as to the understanding of energetic patterns that form life on earth.

Both the Job story and Enheduanna's story suggest that the deities simply have way too much to do, and we take our suffering way too personally. Just wait, it will pass, though we must pay attention and solicit rescue. We are captives of nature, and nature is paradoxical. In the face of the cosmos, we are very tiny indeed.

We can maintain emotional balance in several ways: by keeping a sense of our own innocence as good persons and staying true to ourselves; by expressing our emotions, arguing with the deity, or with fate at least; and by not surrendering to the social definitions of poverty and illness as one's own fault, or as a mark of sin. What also helps is remembering and understanding the vastness of the world, or the greatness of history, and the powers of the cosmos—in the face of how tiny we are, how ultimately inconsequential in the face of life's great principles and patterns. This kind of humility (getting beyond wallowing) is healing and restorative. It does not replace the need for social and ecological justice, given how clearly we can understand recent centuries of human industrialization are impacting climate and habitat. For that, we need the righteous truth-telling outrage that is present in both Enheduanna and the Book of Job.

The lessons in both Enheduanna and Job present psychological steps in dealing with loss. While I did not receive the fortuitous restoration both Enheduanna and Job received—the returning of everything they had lost and more—nevertheless, in my own experiences of grievous loss and near-death illness, healing is a game changer, and the renewed life opens into ever larger vistas and possibilities.

That such an important psychological and theological tale was first told by a woman poet addressing a woman deity is profoundly transformative of how we understand the human past and how it shapes life today. Equally arresting are the differences between the two dramas. Sex, sexual orientation, multiple genders, Satan, and sin—all are certainly in need of reexamination in light of the Sumerian poet's expressing the pre-biblical roots of our civilizations, philosophies, and religious practices.

Allow me to sing her praises: Enheduanna is surely one of the greatest poets who has ever lived.

Praises to the wise people who kept her story alive through thousands of years when her original writing lay hidden under sand.

5

Inanna's Continuing Eruptions

Inanna's Various Aspects in Sumer

Inanna's poetry is full of examples of her intercessions in the cause of justice and on behalf of women's sexual autonomy, of respecting the laws of the cosmos sewn into her own girdle, and of making sure the sustaining plants of the field received nurturing care. She acquired the Eye of Truth after her own ordeal in and resurrection from the underworld. When her lover in his flight was killed by a gang of thugs, she acted decisively to punish the wrongdoers. Her sentences of justice have the restorative quality of turning a past bad deed into a future good one; they are not "an eye for an eye," and instead they effect an alchemical change of the whole situation.

The murder and overthrow of Humbaba, the age-old protector of the cedar forests, outraged the entire council of Sumerian/Babylonian creation gods, which included Inanna/Ishtar. The council elected to kill one of the two offenders, Gilgamesh or Enkidu. Later, both Enki/Ea and Ishtar felt compassion toward the humans when the Wind god set off the great Flood on his own caprice. Ea went so far as to warn his follower Utnapishtim, instructing him how to rescue creatures, his own family, and all the children of the artisans, thus repopulating the earth. Later, Ea rewarded the surviving human couple by situating them in paradise on earth, with eternal life and the privilege of attending the council of the gods.

In her various aspects in the Gilgamesh sojourn, Inanna/Ishtar is also Irnini, keeper of the great cedar Tree of Life, whose base is her crown. This provides a motive for her later rage when Gilgamesh scorns the old rituals that hold city and country together; that weave human life and industry into the life and industry of other beings, of plants and creatures; and that weave women and men into that greater weaving with the sacred marriage and with the rites of death and rebirth. Inanna belongs to the family of deities who judge human actions, deciding who will be reborn and even what tasks will be required of them in their next lives. In Inanna's gift of sacred sex priestesses, which in other cultures have been courtesans (in ancient India, *devadasis*), the graceful arts are blended with the concept of *charis*, which is the complete acceptance of the stranger through erotic satisfactions, and as a way to keep peace. (Obviously this office can function only when there is social agreement of its terms and no exploitation of the poor or helpless.)

We get an idea of Inanna's temple as a place of comfort from this Sumerian poem fragment mentioned earlier: "The mother of the sick lays her child in your arms, the mother of the uprooted [?] . . . in your great hall. You cut the . . . of the weak, you release [?] . . . the weak."

Inanna's compassion and love of family life are evident in the barmaid's advice to Gilgamesh, basically to stop his obsession with his own mortality and instead pay attention to the child clinging to his hand, and give pleasure to the wife in his embrace. It is an ethical position, and sound psychological advice as well. Always, Inanna's ethics are relational.

The snake is perhaps the most subtle form of Inanna in the stories. Snake, as I learned from people in India, is "what animates the earth itself." Through all village goddess practice, the snake is sacred—to Shiva and to many of the goddesses, especially those with erotic qualities, like Shakti, Mariamma, forms of Bhadrakali, and, of course, Kali. Snakes are not allowed to be killed, and they protect small wild groves of trees on every piece of land. Reminders of this are in icons: stone sculptures of upright cobras, sometime with breasts or crowns. As long as these icons stand in the groves, the groves, inhabited by Kali, are protected. For decades, as economic pressures have forced Indian families into urban jobs and away from their land, the icons have been taken to temples and the groves have been cut down, with loss of habitat for wildlife. South Indian ecological activists are fighting to protect the loss of trees, a phenomenon that also threatens the water supply.

The Gilgamesh myth shows us how old and how geographically spread the practice of equating the snake to earth's vitality is. The snake appears in Enheduanna's descriptions of Inanna calling her "First Snake." First Snake hisses venom, the fearsome poison of molten lava writhing down the mountain in a red stream. In Gilgamesh, snakes live with icons in a meadow and are responsible for guiding seekers across the sea of death to the island of Dilmun. In his rage, Gilgamesh destroys these icons and kills the sacred snakes. The boatman finds a way to ferry him across but also states that because of the destruction in the meadow, no one else will ever be allowed to cross the sea of death. In its final appearance, the snake is the one who snatches the plant of eternal life and youth from Gilgamesh, thwarting his last attempt at immortality. It is shedding its skin as it slithers away to its own domain, flower in mouth. The snake—that is to say, the beam of Inanna's vital energy in life—is the keeper of immortality.

In Enheduanna's poem "Inanna and Ebih," the poet tells the story of Inanna as a fierce protector of nature, someone who melts a mountain for one reason: as repeatedly and vehemently stated, the mountain was a form of "paradise" and held itself apart from nature's cycles of abundance, loss, and abundance again. The lion and lamb coexist peacefully (and unrealistically);

the fruit trees are green and continually produce their fruits: abundance without end, life with no need of death and decline, no need of experiencing disaster, transformation, and renewal. Inanna, as nature, obviously opposes this illusion, however comforting it may seem to us human beings.

The great poet used a volcanic episode to teach a moral lesson of ecological justice, exerted by the fierce and fiery goddess in a clash of two worldviews. Many contemporary activists will recognize this situation.

Inanna Continued to Reincarnate in Major Mythology

Enheduanna, the high priestess at Ur, wrote her work exalting the goddess Inanna two or three hundred years before the Gilgamesh myth began, eight hundred before the earliest Sanskritic texts, and eleven hundred before Homer wrote of the war the Greeks fought over the most beautiful Helen of Troy. Enheduanna wrote sixteen hundred years before Sappho said that what is most beautiful is "whatsoever one loves," and eighteen hundred years before the Book of Job was included in Hebrew sacred texts. Inanna's mythologies continued, even as her name and some of her qualities were changed.

In Babylon, she was known by her Akkadian name as the great goddess Ishtar, whose lapis lazuli temple gate was so architecturally stunning that the British later carted it to the British Museum. The goddess changed as patriarchal cultures gradually rose. New patriarchies demanded that female sexuality be restricted to fertility alone, providing an assurance of paternity. Ishtar was to be "faithful" because the patriarchal god was "jealous." During these new eras, men controlled women's bodies. Men became jealous.

Ishtar, with her open sexuality, fell into disrepute as "sinful"; she would come to be called "the Whore of Babylon," gradually diminished from the exalted state of deity Enheduanna, especially, produced for her. Nevertheless, her worship spread to or continued in other places; the Assyrians adored her as Astarte, a name that traveled to the eastern Mediterranean's port cities of Sidon and Tyre. She was A'nat and Ashtoreth in neighboring regions. Later, as Shekinah, she came to be considered the intuitive wisdom of Yahweh. By at least 1200 BCE she had swum up out of the ocean in Greece and been renamed Aphrodite, but however diminished, she retained her beauty, her sexual and romantic intrigues, and her association with the planet Venus.

Aphrodite participated in the story of Helen of Troy, whose life events and qualities parallel Inanna's in a significant number of ways, despite there being many centuries between them. Both Inanna and Helen first loved a farmer, then fell in love with a shepherd. Each was the most beautiful female in her culture, married to a king (Helen was queen of Sparta). Helen carried a torch; Inanna was a torch. Helen was born of an egg; in Babylon, Inanna/Ishtar took the form of an egg in spring.

Queen Helen followed her shepherd lover, Paris, to his hometown of Troy, setting off a ten-year war when her husband gathered his friends in a fleet of ships to bring her back. Once she was returned to her native Sparta, she received an invitation from a woman, Polyxo, to visit her on the island of Rhodes. Thinking this was friendly, Helen went. Polyxo had been widowed during the war and blamed the beautiful Helen for her husband's death. The widow set seven demons (the Furies) onto the queen; they killed her and hung her on a branch of the plane tree. From there her spirit rose into the sky as a goddess; Helen was worshipped at Rhodes for hundreds of years as "Helen of the Trees." This story parallels Inanna's descent myth: the beautiful goddess goes to the realm of a widow, is killed by seven demons, and is hung up on a peg or limb; following this, she rises again and achieves additional powers.

Despite official suppression of the erotic goddess in the newer male-dominated religions, Inanna and her characteristics continued in both literary and folk culture, even while her name changed and the idea of "goddess" increasingly lost authority. Inanna has continued to erupt through the surface of the patriarchies that have denied and suppressed and shamed her. And her eruptions have continued to display her erotic power.

Stories explaining volcanic eruptions as caused by the sexual behavior of the planet the Sumerians adored as Inanna and we adore as Venus continued into the patriarchal eras of Greece and Rome. In Greek mythology, the fire in a mountain was associated with the metallurgy of smiths, specifically Hephaestus, the god of fire and ironwork. Hephaestus married Aphrodite, who didn't love him, and whenever she was unfaithful to him, he flew into a rage, breaking his tools and setting off a volcanic eruption.

In Rome, the god of fire and ironwork was named Vulcan, and he married Venus, the equivalent of the Greek goddess Aphrodite. She didn't love him either, and whenever Venus was unfaithful to Vulcan, his rage created a volcanic eruption. These eruptions initially occurred at Mt. Etna, whose fire was considered his forge.

Vulcan's name was passed down through mythology and the Latin language until it was adopted by early seventeenth-century European geologists, who used the term we know so well: "volcano" comes from the Latin *vulcanus*, meaning "burning mountain."

During the life of Jesus, when Inanna's poetry was more than two thousand years in the past, a sect known as the Gnostics arose in north Africa, which at that time was under the influence of Greece. A man named Simon Magus, a magician and religious philosopher, approached the Apostles with a proposal. He wanted to know how to access Holy Spirit, he said, and would pay them to teach him a method. They laughed and scorned him. Simon then went to a brothel at Tyre (where, as I said, the primary goddess was Astarte) and bought the freedom of a prostitute named Helena. He told her she was a reincarnation of Helen of Troy and would now serve beside him, in trance and channeling spirit, as he preached. The two gathered crowds as they ministered under a plane tree and were worshipped as god and goddess for the next four hundred years, until the state-supported Christian church suppressed them as heretics.

Continuing Inanna's saga, over the next centuries in Europe, Simon and Helena's story was told in outdoor folk theater shows that traveled the countryside. Simon gradually morphed into a German character named Faustus, and he eventually landed in Johann Wolfgang von Goethe's nineteenth-century account as Dr. Faust. Disillusioned with his life's accomplishments in his old age, Dr. Faust sells his soul to Satan in order to attain a second life with youth, love, and beauty, these desires mixing with a longing to reconnect to nature.

In the first half of Goethe's play, Faust seduces a young woman, a pious Christian, and impregnates her. The shame of this causes her to be shunned; she kills her own baby and is executed. Faust, however, continues on his quest. The second half of this long saga, considered the height of German literary accomplishment, includes Faust's marriage to Helen of Troy, whom he has conjured back to life. In the end, however, she returns as a spirit to the underworld along with her beautiful lover, Paris. The complicated accounts of Faust include his various bets and bargains with Mephistopheles, the Satan figure, developed as the "tempter" and reminiscent of the adversary in the Book of Job. Themes of a longing to connect to nature, to experience spirit (erotic power) directly, and to have eternal youth and sexual love with no consequences run throughout the Faust story.

The Gift

My own life was deeply impacted by a version of this story. When I was twenty and very poor, I had been deeply shamed and ostracized as a lesbian by the Air Force. I was living in one room with a hot plate, and no sheets or towels yet. An older man who had been my superior officer, a captain with a daughter my age, decided to "fall in love" with me and seduce me. As part of his seduction attempt, he brought me a gift of a recording of Charles Gounod's opera *Faust*, based on Goethe's play. The sort of misguided sexual "rescue" attempt by an older man could have landed me in a similar situation as the ruined woman in the story; indeed, in my fragile state, it could very easily have led to a life-wrecking tragedy of one kind or another. My body fortunately rejected the captain, but I got to keep the album and fell in love with the opera, both as music and as tragic story. This would eventually lead me to an interest in Helen of Troy, the most beautiful, desirable, and tragic of queens in literature.

A couple of years after I received the captain's gift, Marilyn Monroe, the most beautiful, desirable, and tragic of film queens in the United States and beyond, and already rumored to be John F. Kennedy's mistress, was found dead in her home. This pushed the emotional force even further in me, as the event seemed larger than just news: it seemed epic. Marilyn, the 1950s film goddess of beauty and desire, was emblematic of an era of emergent American sexual freedom. This woman from a lowly station became wife or lover to the most prominent men in her culture—the soldier, the baseball star, the famous playwright, and ultimately the president of the United States. When in 1962 she died at thirty-six, evidently of an overdose, conspiracy rumors began immediately that she had overstepped her station and had been murdered to shut her up.

During this period, I was working as a nurse, receptionist, and lab technician in a doctor's office. Upstairs lived Marie, a glamorous woman (who was mistress of another doctor whose office was on the same floor). She unaccountably disappeared, and a week or so later that doctor sat down in my office just as I was getting ready to leave for the day. In abject grief, that gray-haired man told me that he and Marie had been lovers, that she had immigrated to the United States from Europe, having been forced to give up a baby born out of wedlock. He had moved her into an apartment above his office, where she had lived as his mistress for at least ten years. However, when she recently turned forty, he had told her he didn't want to be involved with her anymore. She thrashed around emotionally for a while, trying this and that, including asking me about my semi-secret lesbian life, and then she swallowed mercury, taking a week to die "in agony," the sorrowful doctor said. He wanted me to tell him why she would have done that. I was speechless. (Women had not yet gathered together and given one another a vocabulary and tongues of courage.) All these tragic stories together had driven a spike into my heart.

What was going on with intensely desired female beauty linked to shame and death? My writing life has been haunted by this theme, and by the time I myself was forty, researching and writing about Helen and, later, Inanna became far more than a compelling literary path for me. This quest is an urgent exploration of why Inanna's stories and those of her pantheon descended over thousands of years as sacred texts, and what was omitted from the originals. What was omitted, and why?

Poets Have Kept Inanna's Spirit Alive

Goethe began his Faust writing in 1772 and continued until final publication in 1829. He based the character on a sixteenth-century German necromancer. Goethe ends his nineteenth-century work with Faust longing for eternal youth, holding only Helen's gown and veil while she herself ascends to the heavens; he concludes his epic poignantly and romantically, with "eternal womanliness" drawing us above and transcending ourselves through love.

Generation after generation poets continue redefining the goddess of love for our age. In the twentieth century, both Amy Lowell and Gertrude Stein wrote short deconstructions of the myth (the latter in "Dr. Faustus Lights the Lights"). H.D. wrote a major reconstruction from a woman's subjective point of view in her epic *Helen in Egypt,* using broad strokes of ancient mythology underpinned with the important men in her own life, including the father of psychoanalysis, Sigmund Freud. In considering the idea that Helen was not to blame for the war—what if she wasn't even there?—the poet challenges the long-standing, underlying social theme of blaming women for "sins" of humanity.

Aside from fragments in the poetry of Edgar Allan Poe, that seedy encounter with the captain who nonetheless left me with the jewel of the *Faust* album was, as I said, my first real intersection with Inanna's great literary tradition. I became curious what "most beautiful woman" could possibly mean, and why this archetype depends heavily on that woman's downfall, degradation, and death.

Deeply impacted by her death at twenty-two, eight years later, immersed in the second-wave grassroots feminist movement, I wrote a poem reclaiming Marilyn's body "for the sake of my own," with an image of placing her bones in a paper sack labeled "the poems of Marilyn Monroe" and then carrying her around the world. Ten years after that, in 1980, inspired by the mythological poems of Charles Olson and *The Black Unicorn* by Audre Lorde, I embarked on my first book-length poem, *The Queen of Wands*. It was a reclamation of the figure of "Helen," woman, queen, and goddess, remythologizing her as a fallen deity who had splintered into a thousand pieces that spread, era upon era, across the globe. In a second book of her epic story, *The Queen of Swords*, I placed her as a middle-class, overly protected woman whose sojourn into a dyke bar results in her becoming bonded with other women; this work drew from my own insights from experiences in the women's movement.

Drawing from their own and related ancestral mythologies, women poets through my lifetime have redescribed the world. Among them, Leslie Marmon Silko used the myth of Yellow Woman with stories of the people and land of Laguna Pueblo. Also with that background, Paula Gunn Allen wrote of Tseche-nako, "Thought Woman" from Acoma origin stories. Audre Lorde named west African deities in her poetry; Luisah Teish, a chief of Ifa-Yoruba tradition, drew from world traditions to create her own eco-mythology. Rita Dove utilized the Demeter-Persephone Greek myth to remythologize real relationships in *Mother Love*; poet-playwright Cherríe Moraga combined themes from Greek Medea with those of La Llorona of Mexican culture. All of them connect everyday lives of women with place, spirit, and a living earth.

Meanwhile, Derek Walcott wrote a new approach to the ancient story of Helen of Troy in his 1990 book-length poem *Omeros*. He divided Helen into two parts, one a child of enslaved people, now a Black waitress named Helen; the other is Helen as the land itself, as the island of Santa Lucia, where he grew up, and by extension she is the land of all of North and South America, fought over by the "gods" as European empire builders, French, English, and Spanish.

As scholars of the literature of Sumer have noted, many components of Sumerian myth were incorporated much later into Genesis: Creation set in a garden paradise full of fruits; humans made of clay plus blood; the mother of life with a snake adviser; a Lord who accepts the offerings of the shepherd but rejects those of the farmer, who subsequently murders the shepherd and is exiled; a great Flood from which only a single man and his wife survive, having rescued "all the animals" in an ark. Biblical poems in the Song of Songs have been compared to Sumerian poems for sensuality and sexually explicit language of lovemaking; for example, "My beloved thrust his hand into the opening / and my inmost being yearned for him. / I arose to open to my beloved" (Marcia Falk, translator).

Parallels between Enheduanna's poetry and the crux of the Book of Job show the Sumerian poet's work as the root of that much later story. While credit for God's character has been attributed to Sumerian gods Ea/Enki, Enlil the Wind, and An the Sky, clearly Inanna contributed quite a bit to the character of God and that of Jesus as well. Inanna's descent to the underworld, in which she is stripped, struck, killed, and hung on a peg for three days and nights, then resurrected, is an obvious precursor to the New Testament Christ story. Another of Inanna's poems declares that bread is flesh and beer is blood, long before the wafer-and-wine communion sacrament became central to

Christian ritual. Sumerian beer, by the way, was dark brownish red, sweetened with figs.

Another similarity with Jesus is obvious: that both have an emphasis on love. As Betty Meador has pointed out, Inanna was a very personal goddess, someone with whom a human of the time could speak; she had a life story of her own, and took human as well as deified form. All this foreshadows that later story of Jesus, the personal god of love, by at least two thousand years. In one striking difference, his love is agape—companionable; sexuality is omitted. By the era of Jesus, the mandate for women was marital fidelity and obedience to husband and father. Gilgamesh foreshadowed this with his scorn for Inanna as a lover who does not provide "eternal love" in her erotic love relationships with males; she is not "faithful." An exception to that is her bond with Ninshubur the female warrior—each woman displays loyalty to the other. At the time of his derision for Inanna's love, Gilgamesh himself had barely begun learning to love.

On the heels of Inanna's descent and return, and a similar saga passed on to her lover Dumuzi, a number of similar myths follow: Demeter and Persephone, Ishtar and Tammuz, Isis and Osiris, and the death of Adonis as grain god. These religious mythologies lasted thousands of years, overlapping with the Jewish, Christian, and Islamic developments. Over eons, the poets weave old stories with new ones, according to the needs of their eras. I'm grateful to the Abrahamic texts for retaining so much of the original poetic work. In the present day, I'm equally grateful to the archaeologists who followed clues in these and other texts to find Troy, then Ur and the other Sumerian cities, and to have some of those cities' wisdom returned to us along with their buried treasures.

With archaeological information about the Stone Age, which has turned up a "great goddess" thesis, it is possible to suppose that for long periods of time cultures center religious belief in only one sex and its rituals, and then a period arises that blends the sexes in a pantheon, until attention shifts toward the other sex and its rituals. Nonbinary and trans people of all orientations both mark and help facilitate these changes. So, if Stone Age peoples created a mother earth religion, which changed into the lively pantheon and origin stories of the Sumerians, then it is a natural turn of human cultural evolution that around 2000 BCE male monotheism was on its way to replacing the rich spectrum of gods that Inanna was part of. This is a broad spiral way of folding all human ritual knowledge into the mix. Over centuries and millennia, the gendered philosophy teaches until some saturation point, then it changes. Therefore, this predicts that we are now deeply into yet another turn of wheel, criticizing and extricating from patriarchy as needed, pushing women's leadership forward, and experiencing massive changes in gender roles, sexual orientation, and identities across the globe.

Having been silenced for generations, women are again finding voice, seeking authority, autonomy, and more—seeking to solve world problems. As world governments turn sharply and defensively to the right, fearfully suppressing women, imprisoning and silencing truth speakers, suppressing reality, it may seem as though humanity is moving backward from this step. However, each new wave of women's collective voices grows in volume and scope: this is an eruption that will not be stilled. Another righteous movement is that for social (including economic) justice, with its unending challenges to the categories of oppression, race, caste, class, and more. Most predictable is the worldwide uproar as human-made climate changes create chaos in every sector. Fear is the worst of human emotions, and in the Sumerian poetry, "even the gods trembled" is an awesome reminder of life-changing events. But in Inanna's stories, love, courage, renewal, intuition, persistence, and connection prevail, again and again.

Inanna is wherever any kind of passion erupts. Inanna is part of all joyful processions, of Mardi Gras, of Carnival, even of the Rose Bowl Parade, as well as any tavern gatherings and parties. Inanna is present in free trade, free choice, with its risk of mistakes or ruinous loss; her justice converts bad deeds into something more positive; she has the capacity (like nature) to reinvent herself. Finally, Inanna sacralizes a remarkable range of genders, with erotic energy permeating the most beautiful, artful, and most mundane of experiences.

Her love is both explicitly sexual and diffusely erotic; it's invitational and nonjudgmental. Her love is compassionate, tender, and familial. Her love is conscious. She advocates for choice, which is not the same as "mandatory inclusion." Her love is not unconditional. She protects women's autonomy, including sexual autonomy, authority, and multiple powers. She protects children, families, and wives. She protects leaders, warriors, and workers, including prostitutes. She creates, protects, and employs cross-gendered people and provides sacred positions for them in her stories and rituals. She inhabits intuition. She is very passionate. Above all, she protects nature and is the animation of nature, an intelligent, formative, relational, interactive, communicative, compassionate, balancing, and co-evolving force in the cosmos. She is in the process of becoming.

Love seems to be a quality of the life force; creatures experience love, joy of life, compassion, and protective ferocity as thoroughly as humans do. The love seems inherent, like an invisible yet detectable radiant beam within nature itself, if we open our hearts to it; and the beam comes and goes. Perhaps this coming and going means that we open and close, or maybe the beam opens and closes too.

Inanna's love is not unconditional. If we are cruel, selfish, or destructive toward nature, she withdraws her protections and her bounty; she withdraws her joyous feelings of goodwill and her tools of survival and renewal.

If we are open-hearted, Inanna's love is as freely given as air; it does not require fidelity, although it does require attention, and practice. Inanna is protective but not jealous or exclusive. She can become furious when scorned or mistreated. She's not faithful either, but available to all. She is generous, joyful, and beautiful. She bestows arts and graces to daily life. This love does not require a pledge of allegiance or martyrdom. Inanna's is a love that is and does; it's not mandatory or enforced; other emotions can play as well, but when we are open to the love, it's there. Or, after a while it's there. Or, it's always there and we fall in and out of connection, so it's up to us. She is steady, unsteady, steady.

Perhaps, in our tumultuous, hazardous times, she needs a contemporary set of *mes*.

Inanna erupts in new forms periodically. In our era, she's overdue.

Notes

Introduction

1   **She wrote three long poems:** Enheduanna's long poems are "Inanna and Ebih," "Lady of Largest Heart," and "The Exaltation of Inanna." The poet also wrote forty-two temple hymns. See Meador, *Princess, Poet, Priestess: The Sumerian Temple Hymns of Enheduanna* (Austin: University of Texas Press, 2009).

1. Inanna, Goddess of Justice

7   **"Inanna and Shukaletuda":** The original version of the Shukaletuda myth is in the invaluable online collection Electronic Text Corpus of Sumerian Literature (hereafter cited by its acronym, ETCSL), maintained by the Oriental Institute at Oxford University. In some cases—most notably, that of Inanna herself—the ETCSL translators use a different spelling ("Inana") than is used in this book. I also draw from my article "Ecology of the Erotic in a Myth of Inanna," *International Journal of Transpersonal Psychology*, 2011.

8   **"Inanna Meets the God of Wisdom":** The ritual passage of cosmic powers from the older generation, represented by Enki, to the younger, represented by Inanna, is perhaps typical or at least recognizable by members of indigenous groups. Paula Gunn Allen, who studied Native American cultures, said that "Inanna Meets the God of Wisdom" reminded her of a Keres (Pueblo people of the American Southwest) annual ritual "battle" either enacted dramatically or told as a story of conflict between people dressed as Winter Spirit and Summer Spirit. Summer Spirit inevitably

wins, as a natural passage of seasonal time with days of cold gradually yielding to days of heat.

8   **Enki graciously had invited:** This version of "Inanna Meets the God of Wisdom" comes from Diane Wolkstein and Samuel Noah Kramer, *Inanna, Queen of Heaven and Earth* (New York: Harper & Row, 1983).

8   **The *mes* (pronounced "mays"):** A list of sixty-four of the *mes* given to Inanna in her drinking rounds with Enki are at this site: https://en.wikipedia.org/wiki/Me_(mythology).

10   **When Enki's assistant sent his weapons:** Possession of all the *mes* involves "not only absolute power but absolute responsibility toward their realization and implementation in the world": Gwendolyn Leick, *A Dictionary of Ancient Near Eastern Mythology* (Abingdon: Routledge, 1991), 117.

15   **Sumerian Culture, Everyday Life, and Connections to India:** Comments about India come from my own observations during four prolonged visits, as well as readings.

17   **Sumerian people loved their family life:** Descriptions of everyday family life are from Joshua J. Mark, "Daily Life in Ancient Mesopotamia," *Ancient History Encyclopedia*, April 15, 2014, https://www.ancient.eu/article/680/daily-life-in-ancient-mesopotamia/.

18   **The icons of deities were placed in tiny huts:** Joshua M. Matson, "Idol Remains: Remnants of the Opening of the Mouth Ritual in the Hebrew Bible," *Studia Antiqua* 12, no. 1 (2013).

20   **"Nona" and "Nana" are names for the planet:** Pupul Jayakar, *The Earth Mother* (San Francisco: Harper & Row, 1990). Her two names for the planet Venus in north India are both similar to "Inanna."

21 **One day goddess Inanna:** Wolkstein and Kramer translated a beautiful version of "The Descent of Inanna into the Underworld" (primarily quoted throughout this passage) in *Inanna, Queen of Heaven of Earth.* As is their "Inanna Meets the God of Wisdom" (cited above), it is replete with all the drama and ritualized repetition of the Sumerian poets. The ending of the descent they use is that of Dumuzi and his sister Geshtinanna taking turns every six months in the underworld.

22 **The two goddesses are sisters:** Ereshkigal's character is perhaps also related to an Asian underworld goddess, Omosi-mama. In a myth from northeastern China written down in the fourteenth century CE, a beautiful young woman is hired by a prince to go into the underworld to retrieve and revive his dead son. Her male assistant drums as the shamaness makes her journey. She takes offerings of cakes, a rooster, and coins. She crosses rivers, confronts and overcomes obstacles (including her own deceased, angry, and estranged husband), until she enters the chamber of the mother of the underworld. Omosi-mama has white hair, protruding eyes, a pointed chin, and red teeth, and is in charge of births as well as deaths. Together with the Sumerian version, these myths clarify the Stone Age roots of conceptions of earth's "underworld" as a womb creating life and effecting reincarnation, birth of all living beings, and fate. *Tale of the Nisan Shamaness: A Manchu Folk Epic* (Seattle: University of Washington Press, 1977), 77-79.

22 **Ereshkigal was in charge:** My understanding of the roles of Ereshkigal and her daughter Nungal comes from reading the Sumerian poetry collection in ETCSL. In "A Hymn to Nungal" therein, Nungal describes herself and names

Inanna as the aunt who favors her: "My own mother, Ereškigala, has allotted to me her divine powers. I have set up my august dais in the nether world, the mountain where Utu rises. I am the goddess of the great house, the holy royal residence. I speak with grandeur to Inana, I am her heart's joy. I assist Nintur at the place of child-delivery (?); I know how to cut the umbilical cord and know the favourable words when determining fates."

23 **At this heart-trembling moment:** The Descent of Inanna may have been based on astronomical observations. That the Sumerians understood Inanna as the planet Venus is evident in such lines in "A Hymn to Inana as Ninegala" (see ETCSL) as: "As you rise in the morning sky like a flame visible from afar, and at your bright appearance in the evening sky." The Sumerians paid close attention to the movements of light in the sky. The habits of the planet Venus are reflected in the mythology of Inanna—that she is the morning and the evening star, and sometimes rides close to the crescent moon, her mother, Ningal. Other planets also appear close to her periodically, especially Mercury (it has been suggested that this planet is Ninshubur, her loyal woman friend). The constellation Taurus (the bull) is sometimes nearby; Enheduanna wrote that "she steps her narrow foot / on the furred back." Venus has an orbit that causes the planet periodically to vanish from our view; during the planet's course, one absence is for three days (another for six weeks). The three-day absence may correspond to the time Inanna's poets decided she was missing while in the below-world in this descent myth.

24 **A variant of the ending:** The Sumerian story of Dumuzi's murder by Old Woman Bilulu is in ETCSL.

28 **The general who led this new move:** Quotes are from Joshua Mark's translation of the myth in his article "The Curse of Agade: Naram Sin's Battle with the Gods," *Ancient History Encyclopedia*, Joshua J. Mark, Aug 2014. https://www.ancient.eu/article/748/the-curse-of-agade-naram-sins-battle-with-the-gods/

2. Gilgamesh, the Rebel Who Turned Against Inanna

35 **Once there was a Sumerian king:** In my retelling of the Gilgamesh story, I am drawing primarily from John Gardner and John Meier, *Gilgamesh: Translated from the Sin-Leqi-Unninni Version* (New York: Vintage, 1985). Their extensive notes, which accompany every page of the translation, are very helpful. (All quotes are from this translation unless otherwise specified.)

36 **Enkidu lived at first:** The Gilgamesh epic was completed long after the earlier mythologies of Inanna; the Sumerian culture had declined, and Babylon was now the center of Mesopotamian urban culture. The seamless weaving of natural elements with urban ones is being dismantled, and the poem records these changes. The goddess, now called by her Akkadian name Ishtar, remains powerful, but she is under siege by the relentless impact of human industry, coupled with patriarchal sexual values.

38 **Furious at this slander of her sacred office:** Ishtar is usually portrayed as in a jealous fit over Gilgamesh's rejection. Author Michael Schmidt, *Gilgamesh: The Life of a Poem* (Princeton: Princeton University Press, 2019), even says she speaks in a childish, manipulative manner with "petulant, little girl's language," 67. However she speaks, she is a

grown-up goddess whose tradition has been rejected by the king. Her anger is justified, and in fact, far from manipulating, she threatens to bring up the dead from the underworld to devour the living if An won't do her bidding. In an earlier Sumerian version, she simply screams. In both versions, he gives in.

41 **Siduri the Barmaid:** Siduri, goddess of ale, is a very appealing character, because she is so human in her alarm at Gilgamesh's anguished appearance, and is so kind to him. In one modern representation of her, she is a mature woman with a long veil down her back, holding a large golden jug: see http://www. anjian.com.au/E12889::160260:Goddess-of-Ale-. Her veil would indicate the containment of a great power. The veil could be drawn around her and her jug to protect others (and herself as well), an indication of the power associated with both the goddess and the drink. Inanna is known as the goddess of beer, although the goddess Ninkasi is credited with the original brewing process.

41 **"Let her delight in your embrace":** The Babylonian text did not include Siduri's advice to Gilgamesh to turn his attention away from morbid obsession to the charms and delights of daily life, of family and its pleasures; see Gardner and Meier, *Gilgamesh*, 214.

47 **"The body that you touched so your heart rejoiced":** A new translation of a cuneiform tablet of Gilgamesh and the Netherworld, an early Sumerian version of what later became the Babylonian Gilgamesh epic, contains specific homosexual imagery. Besides wordplay punning the term for axe with the term for a eunuch who took the receptive part in a sexual act, explicitly genital sex is stated. At the point that Enkidu's ghost arises for one brief reunion of the two friends/lovers, he says to Gilgamesh, "My friend)

the penis that you touched so your heart rejoiced, / grubs devour..(it)..(like an) old garment," 218–19. *Gilgamesh, a New English Version* by Stephen Mitchell (New York: Free Press, 2004), quoting A.R. George, translator, *The Babylonian Gilgamesh Epic: Introduction, Critical Edition, and Cuneiform Texts*, 2 vols. (Oxford: Oxford University Press, 2003). Later scribes and poets rendered this passage as "the *body* you touched," or "the *friend* you touched" (italics mine).

48 **Ishtar appears at least six different times:** There are nearly as many women named in the Gilgamesh myth as there are men, and most of them are aspects of Ishtar. An exception is Ninsun, the mother of Gilgamesh, who appears more than once. She gives advice, promising to adopt his friend Enkidu just as she had adopted all her son's women, interprets Gilgamesh's dreams, and beseeches the Sun god not to lead him astray.

48 **This island was a real place:** Recent archaeological explorations on the island of Bahrain have revealed a temple site, dated around 2300 BCE and dedicated to the water god Ea, as well as a sacred spring. See Geoffrey Bibby, *Looking for Dilmun* (London: Stacey International, 1996).

49 **Irrigation technology, Casey has argued:** Tying together Enki's irrigation constructions with a change in how humans viewed themselves, which have allowed us to attempt to live out a fantasy of perfect eternal life on earth, Rita Casey says, "Specifically, the representation of water as representing an indwelling mystery of potential is redefined by Enki to the power of water understood as providing abundance through the technology of irrigation. This new relationship to water associated with human action in irrigation is conflated with the familiar cultural acts of building and

occupying new structures and thereby links the potency of water and natural law to Enki's human-identified leadership." See Rita Anne Casey, "Inanna and Enki in Sumer: An Ancient Conflict Revisited" (Ph.D. diss., California Institute of Integral Studies, 1998), 299.

Casey asserts that the poetry of Inanna "recognizes the harm caused by the use of discrete consciousness when it masquerades as full awareness. Inannas's response to the dangers of unchecked discrete consciousness is aptly drawn when she destroys Mt. Ebeh [sic]. The rebellion of Mt. Ebeh represents a partial perception in which humans can dominate nature and, in the short turn, imagine that they can isolate themselves from the life-cycles of earth which, in the long run, sustain human existence." Ibid. This echoes Meador's argument (2000).

50 **These three worldviews:** Inanna's descent myth and the Gilgamesh journey describe two very different maturations. Inanna's journey to the underworld, based on long-standing initiation rites, addresses her hubris; she oversteps her authority by trying to sit on her elder sister's chair. Because she has support from her friend, Ninshubur, and because her grandfather looks out for her, she is ritually resurrected to continue her life and reign. In the process she acquires a new power: the Eye of Death—true seeing and true speaking. As a psychodrama, the descent myth works as a process of shedding necessary to acquire greater maturity: speaking truth for justice while remaining compassionate.

Inanna's actions have consequences, which she experiences as her own death, in need of renewal. She goes up against established male authority—the water god and the Sky god—and carves out a place for herself in the cosmic order. She succeeds at this while staying in community with the other deities.

Gilgamesh's journey is also an initiation toward adulthood, intended to give him compassion and the ability to take responsibility for his actions. He fails at this throughout most of his journey, which is largely spent scorning the female powers while consumed with the fear for his own fragility as a mortal who must die. In the process, he overturns the protections that had been in place for nature while remaining in thrall to his emotions and indifferent to what he inflicts.

I see his immaturity projected onto Inanna in descriptions interpreting her as capricious, shallow, grasping, selfish, power-mad, cruel, and (of course) a whore. Except for her stewardship of her sacred sex priestesses, I don't see any of the other qualities in her poetry. She is collaborative, generous, assertive, and protective of both human culture and of nature. Gilgamesh is rejecting everything in her domain, and she reacts by setting the power of the sky upon him. But she is not, in any human female sense, a jealous god.

Or another way to say this: She is seeking decision and voice of authority; she is connecting her heart to her will. He is looking for real courage, and his compassion; he is connecting his will to his heart. And we remain immersed in these journeys.

3. O My Wild, Ecstatic Cow!

56 **Inanna sought to gain the attention:** In *Blood, Bread, and Roses: How Menstruation Created the World* (Boston: Beacon, 1993), I laid out a theory of the importance of menstrua-

tion, and other rites of bleeding, in the development of distinctly human cultural forms and consciousness. Indigenous peoples around the world seem to have extended the imagery of periodic bleeding to all manner of natural forms. These forms include red water; red minerals, such as carnelian and red ocher; and the blood-red appearance of metals in a molten state. More obviously, menstrual ideas and practices were applied to foods such as berries and other fruits and to processes that produce beer, wine, and other mind-altering substances. Sumerian ale was a dark red-brown; it was sweetened with dates and made with (red) emmer wheat. Along with honey cakes, beer was offered to Inanna as a sacred libation.

Blood regulations surrounding women's menstruation were also applied to other aspects of culture, and this is the basis for my interpretation of both the blood in the story of Shukaletuda and (as told in chapter 3) Inanna's reminder of her blood taboo, which serves to save King Sargon's life.

61   **This lively procession was led:** Murray and Roscoe write, "*Kurgarru* . . . are most often identified as servants of Inanna/Ishtar . . . Like the *galli* . . . they perform a kind of war dance, perhaps in a trance state, involving swords, clubs, and blood-letting accompanied by the music of flutes, drums, and cymbals." Stephen O. Murray and Will Roscoe, *Islamic Homosexualities* (New York: New York University Press, 1997), 66.

In the New Year procession to Inanna, and what Gwendolyn Leick calls "ritual acceptance of liminal sexuality under the aegis of the goddess," Leick says, "The climax of the show is the appearance of the kurgarra, who lacerate themselves in an ecstatic frenzy, to the accompaniment of drums." Leicke, *Sex and Eroticism in Mesopotamian Literature* (London: Routledge, 2003), 159.

62   **a ritual dance of Kavady:** I helped film this ritual in Kerala, in a village outside the capital, in 1997. The participants, all men and draped in flower *malas* (thick strings of flowers), carried their heavy wooden burdens as they danced down the road from the Shiva Temple to the Mariamma Temple, about seven kilometers away. Women poured water on them to cool their energies. Many of the men were pierced through the cheeks by small bars that had long metal rods attached; those rods ended in tridents, as though they were fish caught on a spear. This is a healing rite, and something similar is described in poetry of Inanna's processions and also in "A Hymn to Inana as Ninegala." In Sumer, we find "young men fastened in neck-stocks" and dancing before her.

    For a reference to Kavady stocks being originally for the bath of the goddess, see Judy Grahn, *Are Goddesses Metaformic Constructs?: An Application of Metaformic Theory to Menarche Celebrations and Goddess Rituals of Kerala and Contiguous States in South India* (Dissertation, California Institute of Integral Studies, 1999).

63   **Grain says, "Sister, I am your better":** ETCSL.

63   **to see that women amuse themselves:** ETCSL.

63   **She leaned back against the apple tree:** Diane Wolkstein and Samuel Noah Kramer, *Inanna, Queen of Heaven and Earth* (New York: Harper & Row, 1983).

65   **My eager impetuous caresser:** Wolkstein and Kramer, *Inanna, Queen of Heaven and Earth.*

65   **Lady, going to the sweet-voiced cows:** ETCSL.

65 **let me tell you what to say:** Betty De Shong Meador, *Inanna, Lady of Largest Heart* (Austin: University of Texas Press, 2000).

67 **I poured out plants from my womb:** Wolkstein and Kramer, *Inanna, Queen of Heaven and Earth.*

67 **My queen, here is the choice:** Ibid.

67 **Even aside from raising earth energy:** Meador added to Enheduanna's lines "allure, ardent desire / are yours, Inanna" the comment that "Inanna is ready to enter the space between potential or realized lovers and to fill that space with desire because all sexual arousal connects to primary being." See Meador, *Inanna, Lady of Largest Heart*, 159.

68 **astonishing amounts of jewelry:** Sumerian jewelry was undoubtedly used to promote health as well as to describe beauty and status. Energies needing control might have been both benevolent and malevolent, those attaching spirits swirling in the air around them and also those forces carried in their own bodies. Men wore heavier armbands, which were protective, and carried seal rings. Women's body energies especially may have had particular powers. The term "*kuzbu*," which means "overpowering erotic attraction," described the erotic power of the courtesan-priestess Shamhat in the Gilgamesh story. *Kuzbu* is also what Enkidu acquired from Shamhat's body. See John Gardner and John Meier, *Gilgamesh: Translated from the Sin-Leqi-Unninni Version* (New York: Vintage, 1985), 79.

Perhaps *kuzbu* was similar to *ananku*, a concept in ancient India that had both positive and negative effects. Scholar Dianne Jenett says that the Sangam poetry of India reflects worldviews in which "the divine is experienced as immanent, within earthly reality. Ritual practices in which 'the divine is felt to be present' are sensual and ecstatic and 'the psychology of religious awareness is female.' " Dianne Jenett, "Menstruating Women/Menstruating Goddesses: Sites of Sacred Power in Kerala, South India, Sangam Era (100–500 CE) to the Present," in *Menstruation: History and Culture from Antiquity to Modernity*, ed. Andrew Shail (Houndmills: Palgrave Macmillian, 2005), 176–77 (quoting Ram, 64).

Jenett continues: "The Sangam poetry reveals two sources of the sacred: the king and women . . . Ananku is a word used to describe the powers associated with women's sexuality and women's blood which were consistent with, and equivalent to, the divine power in gods, goddesses, forces of nature, animals, warriors and kings." Ibid., 177, quoting Hart, 233.

My poet's ear hears in "*ananku*" a similarity to "Inanna." In any event, these energies would have been regulated through use of amulets, strategic jewelry, and other practices.

69 **Amulets are usually shiny:** In Mesopotamia, the Lilitu were a class of demonic wind spirits believed to affect newborns especially. (Rebecca Lesses, "Lilith," *Jewish Women*, Jewish Women's Archive, p. 2, https://jwa.org/encyclopedia/article/lilith.)

The Atrahasis, a version of the Flood myth written earlier than the completed myth of Gilgamesh, describes how the gods went about controlling the human population after the Flood, as I said in Chapter 2, through the creation of tragedies such as infant death and barrenness, though also through priestess offices forbidding pregnancy and so offering women an escape from mandatory childbirth. At least as early as this account, an incantation against the force of Lilith, believed to cause troubled pregnancies and fatality in babies, was also recorded. Lilitu, a wind goddess or demonic spirit probably taking the form of a human female with wings and owl feet, appears in one of Inanna's stories, nesting in a Huluppu tree that Inanna wanted made into a bed for herself. As a figure able to bring about harm, Lilith has persisted in folk culture for at least four thousand and some scholars say nearly five thousand years, into contemporary times, and many amulets are made today to protect from her influence.

Lilith scholar Deborah Grenn-Scott has observed, "Interestingly, although the Western world has changed drastically since that time, and we speak disparagingly of 'superstitions,' protective amulets warding off Lilith or comparable 'evil' female spirits are still given to pregnant women, placed near the bed of a woman about to give birth or hung in or near the crib of newborn babies in a number of Middle Eastern and North African countries, including Israel, Morocco, Kurdistan and Yemen." Grenn-Scott, *Lilith's Fire: Reclaiming Our Sacred Lifeforce* (San Mateo. Universal Publishers/Lilith Institute, 2000), 39.

Bowls also could serve as amulets. "The liliths are known particularly from the Aramaic incantation bowls from Sassanian and early Islamic Iraq and Iran (roughly 400–800 C.E.). These are ordinary earthenware bowls that ritual specialists or laypeople from the Jewish, Mandaean, Christian and pagan communities, who lived in close proximity in the cities of Babylonia, inscribed with incantations in their own dialects of Aramaic. A drawing of a bound lilith or other demon often appears in the center of the bowl." Lesses, "Lilith."

In contrast to her long sinister reputation, Lilith, as God's first wife and an independent soul who refused to lie beneath Adam, has been redefined by feminists as a positive role model for women.

73　**an intriguing connection to LGBT slang:** I laid out the argument about drag in *Another Mother Tongue: Gay Words, Gay Worlds* (Boston: Beacon, 1984), ch. 4.

73　**Inanna riding in a cart:** Feast of Fools' locations from Will Roscoe's notes, personal communication. He drew from *Sacred Folly: A New History of the Feast of Fools*, by Max Harris (Ithaca: Cornell University Press, 2011).

76　**An interesting new study:** This study is outlined in Gregory S. Paul, "A Preliminary Look at the Possible Relationship Between Mass Consumption of Legal Alcohol and the Existence of Modern Democracy," *The Journal of Psychohistory* 46, no. 2 (2018): 132–46. Inanna's tavern life was full of erotic energy.

77　**As I spin around the lake of beer:** ETCSL.

4. The Woman Who Would Be Job

83　***But he knoweth the way:*** Quotations from the Book of Job in this chapter use the King James Version. I use this translation primarily because I grew up with it and the text is so elegant, written in the high literary age of Shakespeare. In a few places, the committee of churchmen who worked from the Hebrew text to put the KJV together made errors. I have consulted other versions of the Bible—most notably, Robert Alter's *The Hebrew Bible* (New York: W. W. Norton, 2019), which includes extensive commentary—and other translations of the Book of Job. In addition, my colleague, the author Martha Shelley, provided in 2018 her own notes on comparative translations from the Hebrew in

The Jerusalem Bible. Some notes, such as the next one, discuss disparities between the King James Version and the original Hebrew text.

83 ***when he hath tried me, I shall come forth as gold:*** Shelley observes, "The metaphor refers to a metallurgical assay, so the meaning is, 'When he tests me, I shall prove to be gold' " (Shelley notes).

83 ***But he is in one mind:*** "The Hebrew word means he is complete, unchangeable" (ibid.).

83 **steps, yes she steps her narrow foot:** Throughout this chapter, I quote from three long poems by Enheduanna, the high priestess of Ur, as splendidly translated by Betty De Shong Meador in *Inanna, Lady of Largest Heart* (Austin: University of Texas Press, 2000). Working with Sumerian scholars, especially Daniel A. Foxvog, Meador used a combination of artfulness and scholarship coupled with psychological astuteness (she herself was a Jungian psychoanalyst). Meador writes, "After completing the work with Foxvog, I was left alone with boxes of notes on yellow paper from our study ... I took great pleasure struggling with each line, the sometimes contradictory meanings of a word, the broken sentences and missing verses. I approached the task as though I were solving a puzzle" (ibid., 5–6).

85 **At one point while, translating the Sumerian:** Meador observes, "Enheduanna took the new consciousness of the individual, which we see in Akkadian art, and wrote about herself. 'I, I am Enheduanna,' she says. Her poetry was inspired by the most intimate nuances of feeling" (Meador, *Inanna, Lady of Largest Heart,* 48).

Meador became convinced that Enheduanna's accounts of her own overthrow and exile were autobiographical.

Other scholars concur that a political rebellion probably took place in opposition to Enheduanna's father's empire, of which of course she was an integral part, as the highest leader in the civic sphere. The "foe" who exiled her from her temple is named Lugal-anne: "Lugal-anne of Uruk tried to free the provinces from the central rule of the Sargon dynasty" (ibid., 175, 183).

86 **In contrast, the poet or multiple writers:** That the story as told in the Book of Job is essentially a fable was articulated by the medieval Jewish philosopher and rabbi Maimonides in his *Guide for the Perplexed*. See Mark Larrimore, *The Book of Job* (Princeton: Princeton University Press, 2013), 85.

Larrimore says, "The troubled text appears to be corrupted . . . seems not to be of a piece but to have been composed of distinct parts that do not fit together entirely happily" (ibid., 8).

I would say the distinct parts consist of the original passed-down versions of Enheduanna's story and some of her poetry; at some point, these parts were transformed into the tale of a wealthy man, with some characters added, friends whose purpose is arguing with Job about his stalwart position of innocence. Larrimore would seem to agree: "Incongruities between the frame narrative and the poetic dialogue might suggest composite authorship on the largest scale" (ibid., 9).

Looking at the Book of Job as something assembled from multiple authors and fitting together "uneasily," Larrimore distinguishes the "frame narrative" from the "poetic dialogue." Larrimore says, "There may have been an ancient Job, but the story . . . seems to have been crafted later, perhaps even as a riposte to the ancient story" (ibid., 12).

The friends' differing positions on the subject of providence can themselves be parsed. In Archibald MacLeish's *J.B.*, they appear in a more modern context as representative of the voices of Christianity, psychoanalysis, and Marxism (ibid., 87).

In my reading, the fictional friends who argue theology with Job add a novelistic quality to the story, as well as theological points to the subject of suffering. However, my interest remains in the core arguments of Job's and God's, in lines of poetry that echo those of much earlier poet-priestess Enheduanna.

87   **Sarah was probably also a priestess:** Savina Teubal argues convincingly for Sarah and other members of Abraham's retinue being highly educated temple officials in *Sarah the Priestess* (Columbus: University of Ohio Press, 1984).

88   **as are the Hebrew letters z and r:** Shelley notes that the "letters for r (resh) and z (zayin) in Hebrew script look very much alike," so "if the top part of the resh was a little bit short it could easily have been read as zayin, and then subsequent scribes would have dutifully copied the error, down to the present day."

94   *I cry out of wrong . . . there is no judgment*: Martha Shelley comments, "The Jerusalem Bible's concordance translates 'wrong' as violence. 'Judgment' is better rendered as justice" (Shelley notes).

94   **"destroyeth the perfect and the wicked":** "The Hebrew word is 'innocent' rather than 'perfect' " (ibid.).

95   *Wilt thou also disannul my judgment?*: Shelley suggests that in modern English "disannul" should be "disavow" (ibid.).

96   **He discovereth deep things out of darkness:** The verb used in the original Hebrew might be better translated as "uncovers" (ibid.).

96 **I am yours / why do you slay me?:** This phrase does not appear in ETCSL, perhaps something suggesting it was on Foxvog's list of possible interpretations that Betty used.

98 ***He increases the nations, and destroys them:*** Shelley suggests a better translation would be: "He makes nations great, and destroys them; he disperses the nations and consoles them." She explains, "The second clause clearly refers to events like exile, forced relocations, making people into refugees" (Shelley notes).

100 **even the gods are afraid of it:** Robert Gordis's translation is cited in John Hartley, *The Book of Job* (Grand Rapids: Eerdmans, 1988), 529; Gordis also translated "the gods." Robert Alter translates the line as "When he rears up, the gods are frightened, / when he crashes down, they cringe" (Alter, *The Hebrew Bible*, 3:576).

100 **For what is the hope of the hypocrite:** Shelley observes, "Hypocrite is one of the minor definitions of the word, which more predominantly means profane, ungodly, rather than the way we use the word hypocrite today. And the word gained actually means gained by violence, most usually robbed" (Shelley notes).

100 **no thought can be withholden:** The Hebrew noun might actually be better translated as "plan" or "scheme" (ibid.)

103 **"evil silt":** ETCSL.

104 **"clay bowl":** ETCSL.

104 **pressed the dagger's teeth into its interior:** ETCSL.

108 **So God and Inanna are both credited:** In "The Exploits of Ninurta," another myth of a god fighting a mountain-monster (available at ETCSL), the meaning of Inanna's fight with Mt. Ebih is made even more clear. Ninurta is

one of Inanna's lovers, a young hero god lionized by her when she is older. He was later credited with invention of the plow, and with poetic instructions that apparently served as an early farmers' almanac. Ninurta "fights" Asag, a disease-causing monster that has set the rivers to boiling. Asag meets Ninurta's charge with an "army" consisting of stones and plants. Ninurta slays them all, "smashes their heads," spreads "gore," cleans "blood" from his clothing, and ultimately piles up the "corpses" to build walls that redirect the water and enable irrigation.

On a day that "became like pitch" the hero marches toward the monster: "the Asag fell on Ninurta, son of Enlil. Like an accursed storm, it howled in a raucous voice; like a gigantic snake, it roared at the Land. It dried up the waters of the mountains, dragged away the tamarisks, tore the flesh of the Earth and covered her with painful wounds. It set fire to the reedbeds, bathed the sky in blood, turned it inside out; it dispersed the people there. At that moment, on that day, the fields became black potash, across the whole extent of the horizon, reddish like purple dye—truly it was so!" ("The Exploits of Ninurta").

The hero had been told that Asag causes people to choke, scrubs the earth raw, and chases the wild donkeys before it. "Its terrifying splendour sends the dust into clouds, it causes a downpour of potsherds." The "downpour of potsherds" would be lava cinders, which are quite sharp.

After Asag is "killed" (i.e., after the lava cools), Ninurta announces, "From today forward, do not say Asag: its name shall be Stone": a fitting renaming of lava. He then renames his mother, Ninmah, incorporating "Asag" into her new name. That appellation, Ninhursag, can be translated as "Lady Stony-Earth" or "Lady Mountain." Even though Ninurta lavishly praises the earth mother for various life-giving achievements, the new title "stony-earth" is a diminishing of the creation powers carried by the widespread earth goddess named "Mah." Ninurta decrees for his mother a place of fecundity similar to the paradisial description of Mt. Ebih. Then Ninurta is approached by the creatrix Aruru, who tells him he must assign tasks, as I described in chapter 3, and "fix the fate" of the stones he has captured, or as Aruru says, "warriors you have killed".

After I read "The Exploits of Ninurta," I understood his "killing" of the monster Asag as a description of what we would today call vulcanism. The details in this tale reveal the similarity to Inanna's attack on Mt. Ebih, and it became self-evident both accounts are describing volcanic episodes. Both also use ferocious battle imagery throughout. Other indigenous people have also described volcanoes in terms of battle. For example, the indigenous Klamath people who lived on Mt. Mazama, whose post-explosion caldera became Crater Lake in Oregon, have continued retelling their mythology of the event that occurred thousands of years ago. They describe the volcanic activity in terms of a ferocious battle between two gods.

Sumerian scholars have interpreted Asag as a monster, a dragon, a demon, or even a tree. Perhaps it's not surprising then that various interpretations by biblical scholars of Leviathan (as a crocodile, for instance) do not recognize the volcanic imagery; instead, even recent, fresh translations continue to use the metaphor of "beast." Lava can resemble gigantic scales. In some volcano flows, the lava seeps along in successive waves that slightly overlap and cool next to one another, with indentations that seem like seams but are not. They resemble giant gray scales or, as Robert Alter has translated God's description of Leviathan: "His back is rows of shields, / closed with the tightest seal. / Each touches against the next, / no breath can come between them. / Each sticks fast to the next, / locked together, they will not part" (Alter, *The Hebrew Bible*, 3:575).

Maybe the connections fell into place for me because I grew up around old volcanoes in the American Southwest, hiking across the sharp cinder–strewn lava fields as well as witnessing the caldera of Crater Lake in Oregon, and the "melting" of a huge section of the north flank of Mt. Saint Helens during its 1980 eruption. More recently, pictures, videos, and friends' descriptions of the lava of Hawaii's Mt. Kilauea slithering snakelike in hissing red tongues of molten rock into the sea also aided in my perceptions of what the ancient poets were seeing. Betty Meador catches the fiery disposition of Inanna with wonderful dramatic lines. The ETCSL translation includes the image of Ebih "melted like a vat of sheep's fat" and the mountain's shape as "like a pot" (a caldera).

In a paper, Fumi Karahashi draws a connection between the two deities and their battles with mountains. Although I don't agree with her interpretations of the deities, she drew my attention to the Ninurta myth. See Karahashi, "Fighting the Mountain: Some Observations on the Sumerian Myths of Ninurta and Inanna," *Journal of Near Eastern Studies* 63, no. 2 (2004): 111–18.

111 ***And the Lord turned the captivity of Job***: Shelley comments, " 'Turned the captivity' is an old Hebrew metaphor that the King James Bible translates literally—it actually means 'restored the fortunes' " (Shelley notes).

111 **Where does morality fit with this?**: Neither Inanna's poet Enheduanna nor the later figure of Job accepts that they have done wrongdoing. Yet surely it is their sense of

righteousness that increases their suffering. The emotions of loss are bad enough; the sense of having been wrongly targeted increases the pain. The teaching of humility in the face of the enormity of the cosmos eases this part of the loss, my own experience tells me. On the other hand, in the story "The Cursing of Agade," a king so displeases the gods of nature that they withdraw their benevolent presence, and his entire domain and everyone living in it crashes in a horror of destruction.

112 **The Sumerians' view of Inanna:** The fragment about the mother laying a sick child in the arms of the goddess is from "Hymn to Inana as Ninegal" from ETCSL.

113 **Satan as a supernatural force:** The concept of Satan seems to have evolved over centuries to include all manner of explanations for nearly anything that might trigger fear, though it has come to mean that which must be excluded, as "demonic."

115 *Then let my wife grind unto another:* Shelley notes that this might sound as though it's about sex in modern English, but it literally means that the wife is "grinding grain for another guy" (Shelley notes).

117 **To build a house / construct the women's rooms:** ETCSL.

118 **Other Sumerian names for androgynous:** Will Roscoe, personal communication and unpublished chart, "Priests of the Goddess: Mediterranean-Mesopotamia-India-Southeast Asia." Some of the information is in "Priests of the Goddess: Gender Transgression in Ancient Religion," *History of Religions* 35, no. 3 (Feb., 1996): 195–230.

Also, Gwendolyn Leick observes that "it is in Inanna's power to assign sexual identity": Leick, *Sex and Eroticism in Mesopotamian Literature* (London: Routledge, 2003), 159. Enheduanna says Inanna causes "priest to become woman / priestess to become man" (Meador, *Inanna, Lady of Largest Heart*, 102), as though the poetry describes sacred *offices* rather than only sexual "identity," as we might say.

119 **Nothing like sin or disapproval:** "Hymn to Inana," "When she had removed the great punishment from her body, she invoked blessings upon it; she caused it to be named the *pilipili*. She broke the spear and as if she were a man . . . gave her a weapon." ETCSL.

5. Inanna's Continuing Eruptions

131 **Inanna's Various Aspects in Sumer:** That a goddess or god has "aspects" is reflected in India, where devotees explain that very diverse deities are "avatars" of Ram, for instance, or "sisters" to Bhadrakali.

135 **Aphrodite participated in the story:** An excellent resource on this subject is Bettany Hughes, *Helen of Troy: Goddess, Princess, and Whore* (New York: Alfred A. Knopf, 2005). It explores mythology and history and links Spartan mythology with the later Gnostic writings of Helena and Simon.

135 **Helen was born of an egg:** Helen's egg continues to exist, given special honor in various churches. Inanna may also have had ritually used eggs, intricately adorned. One, a gorgeous ostrich eggshell, possibly a libation vessel, painted gold and with a rim of lapis, shell, and red limestone, was found in an Inanna temple at Nippur. See *Treasures from the Royal Tombs of Ur*, edited by Richard L. Zettler and Lee Horne (Philadelphia: University of Pennsylvania Press, 1998). The Book of Job contains a passage about the ostrich, castigating the mother bird for its habit of nesting on

the ground. Enheduanna's poetry contains no such reference, but many lines are missing from her text.

137 **Dr. Faust sells his soul to Satan:** Philip Mason Palmer and Robert Pattison More, T*he Sources of the Faust Tradition* (New York: Haskell House, 1965), list Simon Magus as one of three probable forerunners of Faust stories. They quote at length from accounts of Simon Magus as "a conjurer and blowhard" who challenged the disciple Peter to contests of miracles, stories kept alive in accounts by Christian writers. Christopher Marlowe wrote his play no earlier than 1588, but earlier puppet plays in Germany carried forward the story of a Dr. Faustus conjuring all manner of devils and demons to fulfill his desire for eternal youth (ibid., 279 ff).

140 **Generation after generation poets continue:** H.D. gave Helen a deeply interior, subjective voice in a broad mythological landscape. She blended contexts and characters from contemporary life with Greek, Roman, and Egyptian mythologies. Thirty years later, Walcott used both a personal, intricate voice and the broadest mythological and historic strokes in addressing both personal and communal oppressions. He transformed the mythic Homeric characters into Caribbean fishermen. Walcott drew on African and African-Caribbean mythology, and guided himself on an ancestral journey. He used the voice of the poet as "Omeros" as well as his own voice.

I too blended mythologies and contemporary life, setting my play in an underground lesbian bar. In my rendition, I was interested in Ereshkigal's voice and in the role of an "underworld mother" as a positive, empowering change agent. Most poets use stories for both personal and communal healing, as Enheduanna did, if not also the poets of Gilgamesh.

In my play *The Queen of Swords*, Ereshkigal says to Inanna:

I will suffer too, to birth you
to transform and finally release you . . .
you will think of me
as she who bore you to your new
and lawful place of rising
took the time and trouble
just to get you there
so you could moan Inanna, you could cry
and everyone you ever were
could die.

In *Inanna, Lady of Largest Heart*, Betty Meador identified four new archetypes for women: Lover, Warrior, Priestess, and Androgyne. She and Sylvia Brinton Perera, among others, have described the descent myth as a psychological tool. Among many others, the writings of Diane Wolkstein, Meador, Starhawk, and writers collected in *Inanna's Ascent: Reclaiming Female Power*, an anthology edited by Trista Hendren, Tamara Albanna, and Pat Daly (self-published, 2018), show that women are already using Inanna's poetry to re-mythologize themselves.

142 **As scholars of the literature of Sumer:** Marcia Falk, *Song of Songs: Love Lyrics of the Bible* (New York: Harcourt Brace Jovanovich, 1977). In *For the Love of God: The Bible as an Open Book* (New Brunswick: Rutgers University Press, 2007), poet Alicia Suskin Ostriker suggests the biblical Song of Songs may stem from the love poems of Inanna and Dumuzi (15). In both, the lover is a shepherd and a king. The

female lover is a garden, an apple tree is mentioned, and both sets of poems are lushly romantic and erotic.

According to author Chana Bloch, "sex is no sin in the Old Testament" (quoted in ibid., 14). Ostriker discusses sex between men and women as pleasurable and as sacred, not only in support of matrimony, but including the embrace of God with Shekhinah on Friday nights as well. Ostriker confirms the egalitarian values in biblical love poetry, observing, "What is extraordinary in the Song is precisely the absence of structural and systemic hierarchy, sovereignty, authority, control, superiority, submission, in the relationship of the lovers and their relationship to nature" (Ostriker, *For the Love of God*, 27).

Bibliography

Alter, Robert. *The Hebrew Bible*. 3 vols. New York: W. W. Norton, 2019.

Bhattacharyya, Narendra Nath. *History of the Sakta Religion*. 2nd ed. New Delhi: Munshiram Manoharlal Publishers, 1996.

Bibby, Geoffrey. *Looking for Dilmun*. 2nd ed. London: Stacey International, 1996.

Black, Jeremy, Graham Cunningham, Eleanor Robson, and Gabor Zolyomi. *The Literature of Ancient Sumer*. Oxford: Oxford University Press, 2006.

Casey, Rita Anne. "Inanna and Enki in Sumer: An Ancient Conflict Revisited." Ph.D. diss., California Institute of Integral Studies, 1998.

Dashu, Max. "The Gnostic Goddess, Female Power, and the Fallen Sophia." 2010, accessed 2018. www.academia.edu.

Downes, Jeremy M. *The Female Homer: An Exploration of Female Epic Poetry*. Newark: University of Delaware, 2010.

Dyr, Peter. *The Epic of Gilgamesh, the Teachings of Siduri and How Siduri's Ancient Advice Can Help Guide Us to a Happier Life*. Self-published, 2013.

ETCSL (Electronic Text Corpus of Sumerian Literature). Oriental Institute, Oxford University (orinst.ox.ac.uk). http://etcsl.orinst.ox.ac.uk/cgi-bin/etcsl.cgi?text=t.1.6.2#. (As indicated in the notes, this site, which I accessed continually in 2019, was an invaluable source for the texts of "Inanna and the Errant Gardener" and other tales and poems discussed in this book. Among the major subpages of the website I consulted were "The Exploits of Ninurta," "Enki's Literature," "Inanna's Literature," and "Enlil's Literature.")

Fisch, Harold, trans. *The Jerusalem Bible: The Holy Scriptures*. Jerusalem: Koren, 2000.

Foster, Benjamin R. Translator and editor. *The Epic of Gilgamesh*. New York: W. W. Norton, 2001.

Gardner, John, and John Meier. *Gilgamesh: Translated from the Sin-Leqi-Unninni Version*. New York: Vintage, 1985.

George, Andrew, trans. *The Epic of Gilgamesh: The Babylonian Epic Poem and Other Texts in Akkadian and Sumerian*. London: Penguin, 2000.

Goethe, Johann Wolfgang von. *Faust: Parts One and Two*. Translated by George Madison Priest. Chicago: Encyclopedia Britannica, 1941.

Grahn, Judy. *Another Mother Tongue: Gay Words, Gay Worlds*. Boston: Beacon, 1984.

———. "Are Goddesses Metaformic Constructs? An Application of Metaformic Theory to Goddess and Menarche Rituals in Kerala, South India." Ph.D. diss., California Institute of Integral Studies, 1999.

———. *Blood, Bread, and Roses: How Menstruation Created the World*. Boston: Beacon, 1993.

———. "Ecology of the Erotic in a Myth of Inanna." *International Journal of Transpersonal Psychology*. 2011.

———. *The Queen of Swords*, in *The Judy Grahn Reader*. San Francisco: Aunt Lute Press, 2009.

Grenn-Scott, Deborah. *Lilith's Fire: Reclaiming Our Sacred Lifeforce*. San Mateo: Universal Publishers/The Lilith Institute, 2000.

Harris, Rivkah. "Inanna-Ishtar as Paradox and a Coincidence of Opposites," *History of Religions* 30, no. 3 (1991): 261–78.

Hartley, John E. *The Book of Job: The New International Commentary on the Old Testament.* Grand Rapids: Eerdmans, 1988.

H.D. *Helen in Egypt: Poetry.* New York: New Directions, 1974.

Hendren, Trista, Tamara Albanna, and Pat Daly, editors. *Inanna's Ascent: Reclaiming Female Power.* Self-published, 2018. (Also available online at A Girl God Anthology, www.thegirlgod.com.)

Hoeller, Stephen A. *Gnosticism: New Light on the Ancient Tradition of Inner Knowing.* Wheaton: Quest Books, 2001.

Homer. *The Iliad of Homer.* Translated by Richmond Lattimore. Chicago: University of Chicago Press, 1951.

Hughes, Bettany. *Helen of Troy: Goddess, Princess, and Whore.* New York: Alfred A. Knopf, 2005.

Induchudan, V.T. *The Secret Chamber: An Historical, Anthropological, and Philosophical Study of Kodungallur Temple.* Thrissur: Chochin Devaswom Board, 1969.

Jacobsen, Thorkild. *The Harps That Once—: Sumerian Poetry in Translation.* New Haven: Yale University Press, 1987.

Jayakar, Pupul. *The Earth Mother: Legends, Ritual Arts, and Goddesses of India.* San Francisco: Harper & Row, 1990.

Jenett, Dianne. "Menstruating Women/Menstruating Goddesses: Sites of Sacred Power in Kerala, South India, Sangam Era (100–500 CE) to the Present." In *Menstruation: History and Culture from Antiquity to Modernity*, edited by Andrew Shail. Houndmills: Palgrave Macmillan, 2005.

Karahashi, Fumi. "Fighting the Mountain: Some Observations on the Sumerian Myths of Ninurta and Inanna." *Journal of Near Eastern Studies* 63, no. 2 (2004). DOI: 10.1086/422302.

Kasak, Enn, and Raul Veede. "Understanding Planets in Ancient Mesopotamia." *Folklore* 16 (2001).

Kovaks, Maureen Gallery. *The Epic of Gilgamesh*. Stanford: Stanford University Press, 1985.

Kramer, Samuel Noah. *The Sumerians: Their History, Culture, and Character*. Chicago: University of Chicago Press, 1971.

Larrimore, Mark. *The Book of Job*. Princeton: Princeton University Press, 2013.

Lerner, Gerda. *The Creation of Patriarchy*. New York: Oxford University Press, 1986.

Lesses, Rebecca. "Lilith." *Jewish Women: A Comprehensive Historical Encyclopedia*. Jewish Women's Archive. March 20, 2009, accessed August 14, 2019. https://jwa.org/encyclopedia/article/lilith.

Leick, Gwendolyn. *A Dictionary of Ancient Near Eastern Mythology*. Abingdon: Routledge, 1991.

———. *Sex and Eroticism in Mesopotamian Literature*. London: Routledge, 2003.

MacLeish, Archibald. *J.B.* Boston: Houghton Mifflin, 1958.

Mark, Joshua J. "The Atrahasis Epic: The Great Flood and the Meaning of Suffering." *Ancient History Encyclopedia*. March 6, 2011. https://www.ancient.eu/article/227/the-atrahasis-epic-the-great-flood--the-meaning-of/

———. "Daily Life in Ancient Mesopotamia." *Ancient History Encyclopedia*. April 15, 2014. https://www.ancient.eu/article/680/daily-life-in-ancient-mesopotamia/.

———. "The Ludlul-Bel-Nimeqi: Not Merely a Babylonian Job." *Ancient History Encyclopedia*. March 6, 2011. https://www.ancient.eu/article/226/.

Matson, Joshua M. "Idol Remains: Remnants of the Opening of the Mouth Ritual in the Hebrew Bible." *Studia Antiqua* 12, no. 1 (2013). https://scholarsarchive.byu.edu/studiaantiqua/vol12/iss1/3.

McGuire, Laurie. *Helen of Troy: From Homer to Hollywood*. Chichester: Wiley-Blackwell, 2009.

Meador, Betty De Shong. *Inanna, Lady of Largest Heart: Poems of the Sumerian High Priestess Enheduanna*. Austin: University of Texas Press, 2000.

———. *Princess, Poet, Priestess: The Sumerian Temple Hymns of Enheduanna*. Austin: University of Texas Press, 2009.

———. *Uncursing the Dark: Treasures from the Underworld*. Wilmette: Chiron Press, 1994.

Mitchell, Stephen. *Gilgamesh: A New English Version*. New York: Free Press, 2004.

Moffet, Joe. *The Search for Origins in the Twentieth Century Long Poem: Sumerian, Homeric, Anglo-Saxon*. Morgantown: West Virginia University Press, 2007.

Murray, Stephen O., and Will Roscoe. *Islamic Homosexualities: Culture, History, and Literature*. New York: New York University Press, 1997.

Nowak, Margaret C., and Stephen W. Durrant. *The Tale of the Nisan Shamaness: A Manchu Folk Epic*. Seattle: University of Washington Press, 1977.

Ostriker, Alicia Suskin. *For the Love of God: The Bible as an Open Book*. New Brunswick: Rutgers University Press, 2007.

Pagels, Elaine. *The Gnostic Gospels*. New York: Vintage, 1979.

Palmer, Philip Mason, and Robert Pattison More. *The Sources of the Faust Tradition: From Simon Magus to Lessing.* New York: Haskell House, 1965.

Paul, Gregory S. "A Preliminary Look at the Possible Relationship Between Mass Consumption of Legal Alcohol and the Existence of Modern Democracy: Evidence That the Latter Requires the Former." *The Journal of Psychohistory* 46, no. 2 (2018): 132–46.

Perera, Sylvia Brinton. *Descent of Inanna: A Way of Initiation for Women,* Toronto: Inner City Books, 1981.

Schmidt, Michael. *Gilgamesh: The Life of a Poem.* Princeton and Oxford: Princeton University Press, 2019.

Teubal, Savina J. *Sarah the Priestess: The First Matriarch of Genesis.* Columbus: University of Ohio Press, 1984.

Vanamali. *Shakti: Realm of the Divine Mother.* Rochester: Inner Traditions, 2008. (Originally published in India under the title *Sri Devi Lila: The Play of the Divine Mother* by Aryan Books, 2006.)

Wade, Lizzie. "South Asians Are Descended from a Mix of Farmers, Herders, and Hunter-Gatherers, Ancient DNA Reveals." Sciencemag.org, April 18, 2018. https://www.sciencemag.org/news/2018/04/south-asians-are-descended-mix-farmers-herders-and-hunter-gatherers-ancient-dna-reveals

Walcott, Derek. *Omeros.* New York: Farrar, Straus and Giroux, 1990.

Wolkstein, Diane, and Samuel Noah Kramer. *Inanna, Queen of Heaven and Earth: Her Stories and Hymns from Sumer.* New York: Harper & Row, 1983.

Yamauchi, Edwin M. "The Descent of Ishtar, the Fall of Sophia, and the Jewish Roots of Gnosticism." *Tyndale Bulletin* 29 (1978): 143–75.

Index

Abel (Biblical), 88

Abraham (Biblical), 87, 88–89, 124, 166n87

Abrahamic religions, 50, 85, 88, 143
 See also Christianity; Islam; Judaism

Achilles, 47

Adam (Biblical), 116, 122, 161n69

Adonis, 24, 143

Africa, 3, 76, 105, 114, 137, 141, 161n69, 173n140

Akkad, 28, 30, 48, 71, 84, 87
 Ishtar/Inanna in, 35, 134, 153n38, 164n85

Akkadian mythology, 3

Allen, Paula Gunn, 141, 149n8

Alter, Robert, 163n83, 167n100

American poetic mythology, 3

amulets, 68–69, 72, 160n68, 161n69

An, 19, 60, 91, 101, 117, 121, 124, 142, 153n38

ananku, 160n68

A'nat, 135

Anunnaki, 17, 23, 99

Aphrodite, 75, 135–36

Apostles, 137

archaeology, 15, 48, 68, 84, 143, 155n48

Aruru, 43, 167n108

Asag, 167n108

Ashtoreth, 135

Assyria, 135

Astarte, 135, 137

Atrahasis, 161n69

Attis, 24

Ayoub, 85

Acknowledgments

First, my gratitude to Julie Enszer for sparking a place for me to write this book, then working so hard on it, and then collaborating with Nightboat Books for expanded exposure. And gratitude to Stephen Motika at Nightboat for taking it on, and to Nieves Guerra for such a splendid book design.

My eternal gratitude to Betty De Shong Meador for her rendering of Enheduanna's poems in her book, *Lady of Largest Heart*.

Gratitude to Martha Shelley for her research notes and helpful feedback; to Anya De Marie for her response and for the subtitle; to D'vorah Grenn for persistent support, early editing, and references; and to Will Roscoe for his invaluable scholarship on the *kurgarra*. Thanks to the initial copy editor Trent Duffy, proofreader Amy Haejung, and Gregory Gajus, Rita Casey, Dawn McGuire, Angela Hume, and Joellen Hiltbrand for early editing and/or thoughtful response. Thanks to students in the Women's Spirituality MA programs at NCOC and ITP for listening to my earliest versions. To Cosi Fabian for clarifying and honoring sacred prostitution, and to Glenn Hartelius for publishing "Ecology of the Erotic in a Myth of Inanna" in the *International Journal of Transpersonal Psychology*.

Finally, and most importantly, to my dyke-spouse Kris Brandenburger and our friend Dianne E. Jenett for giving me shelter, emotional and physical support, and great editing and feedback.

Photo Credit: Irene Young

Judy Grahn is an internationally known poet, author, and cultural theorist. *Eruptions of Inanna* is her seventeenth published book. An early gay activist who walked the first picket of the White House for gay rights in 1965, she later co-founded Gay Women's Liberation and the Women's Press Collective. Her subjects range from LGBT history and mythology to feminist critiques of current crises, new origin theories of inclusion, what makes us human, taking antiracism personally, and stories of how to engage with creature-minds and spirits. She writes about and teaches her own poetry and also that of Sumerian poets interacting with goddess Inanna.

Dr. Grahn holds a PhD in Integral Studies/Women's Spirituality and researched her dissertation in south India. She has received many awards and honors, including Grand Marshall of two Gay Pride parades, several lifetime achievement awards including the Fred Cody Award for Literature and Social Service, two American Book Awards, a Stonewall Award, two Lambda Literary Awards, and the Demeter Award for Leadership in Women's Spirituality from the Association for the Study of Women and Mythology. In 2019 she was inducted into the Tennessee Williams Festival Saints and Sinners Hall of Fame. Publisher's Triangle established "The Judy Grahn Nonfiction Award" in 1996. She is currently Associated Distinguished Professor at the California Institute of Integral Studies' PhD program in Transpersonal Psychology.

Nightboat Books

Nightboat Books, a nonprofit organization, seeks to develop audiences for writers whose work resists convention and transcends boundaries. We publish books rich with poignancy, intelligence, and risk. Please visit nightboat.org to learn about our titles and how you can support our future publications.

The following individuals have supported the publication of this book. We thank them for their generosity and commitment to the mission of Nightboat Books:

Kazim Ali
Anonymous (4)
Jean C. Ballantyne
Will Blythe
The Robert C. Brooks Revocable Trust
Amanda Greenberger
Anne Marie Macari
Elizabeth Madans
Elizabeth Motika
Benjamin Taylor
Jerrie Whitfield & Richard Motika

Nightboat Books gratefully acknowledges support from the New York City Department of Cultural Affairs in partnership with the City Council, the New York State Council on the Arts Literature Program, and the Topanga Fund, which is dedicated to promoting the arts and literature of California.

Sinister Wisdom

Sinister Wisdom is a multicultural lesbian literary & art journal that publishes four issues each year. Publishing since 1976, *Sinister Wisdom* works to create a multicultural, multi-class lesbian space. *Sinister Wisdom* seeks to open, consider, and advance the exploration of community issues. *Sinister Wisdom* recognizes the power of language to reflect our diverse experiences and to enhance our ability to develop critical judgment, as lesbians evaluating our community and our world.

Editor and Publisher: Julie R. Enszer, PhD

Former editors and publishers:
Harriet Ellenberger (aka Desmoines)
    and Catherine Nicholson (1976–1981)
Michelle Cliff and Adrienne Rich (1981–1983)
Michaele Uccella (1983–1984)
Melanie Kaye/Kantrowitz (1983–1987)
Elana Dykewomon (1987–1994)
Caryatis Cardea (1991–1994)
Akiba Onada-Sikwoia (1995–1997)
Margo Mercedes Rivera-Weiss (1997–2000)
Fran Day (2004–2010)
Julie R. Enszer & Merry Gangemi (2010–2013)

Subscribe online: www.SinisterWisdom.org

Sinister Wisdom is a U.S. nonprofit organization; donations to support the work and distribution of *Sinister Wisdom* are welcome and appreciated.